Jackie Weaver is Chief Officer of the Cheshire Association of Local Councils. In December 2020 she acted as facilitator at a meeting of the Handforth Parish Council. Since a recording of the meeting went viral in February 2021, Jackie has found herself catapulted to fame – she has been immortalised in sponge cake, had her face and catchphrases printed on T-shirts and fridge magnets and cut her first dance track. Jackie recently launched her chart-topping podcast, Jackie Weaver Has the Authority, which has hosted a wide range of guests including Jack Whitehall, Anton Du Beke and Jeremy Vine.

JACKIE WEAVER

You Do Have the Authority Here!

CONSTABLE

CONSTABLE

First published in Great Britain in 2021 by Constable

1 3 5 7 9 10 8 6 4 2

Copyright © Jackie Weaver, 2021

Written by Emma Marriott

The moral right of the authors has been asserted.

A CIP catalogue record for this book
is available from the British Library.

ISBN: 978-1-40871-602-1 (hardback)

Typeset in Bembo by Hewer Text UK Ltd, Edinburgh
Printed and bound in Great Britain by Clays Ltd, Elcograf, S.p.A.

Papers used by Constable are from well-managed forests and other responsible sources.

Constable
An imprint of
Little, Brown Book Group
Carmelite House
50 Victoria Embankment
London EC4Y 0DZ

An Hachette UK Company
www.hachette.co.uk

www.littlebrown.co.uk

To all the unsung heroes and heroines of the local council world for their driving enthusiasm and tireless efforts and to my husband for his endless kindness and patience.

Contents

1. The Meeting of the Handforth Parish Council   1

2. Meeting Etiquettes: Dos and Don'ts   20

3. How to Get Things Done   31

4. Dealing with Difficult People   42

5. You Have the Authority   55

6. Be Assertive. Be Heard. Be Human.   67

7. Keep Calm and Press Mute on the Noise   78

8. Dealing with Adversity (and Loss)   92

9. A Commonsense Approach   105

10. Be Comfortable In Your Own Skin   116

11. The Final Word   129

Chapter One

The Meeting of the Handforth Parish Council

Dramatis personae:

Jackie Weaver/Britney Spears: chief officer of the
    Cheshire Association of Local Councils
Brian Tolver: Handforth parish council (PC) self-elected
    clerk and chairman
Aled Brewerton: vice-chair
Aled Brewerton's dad: father to Aled
Barry Burkhill: councillor and mayor of the borough
Cynthia Sampson: councillor
John Smith: councillor and chairman elected for the
    meeting
Sue Moore: councillor
Peter Moore, David Pincombe, Roger Small, Ian Ball and
    others: members of the public

Jackie Weaver is inviting you
to a scheduled Zoom meeting

Topic: The Handforth parish council planning and environment committee. Two councillors have called a meeting of other councillors and members of the public, all joining from their homes around the Cheshire East area. Jackie Weaver is faciliating the meeting.

Time: 7 p.m. 10 December 2020

Please wait for the host to start this meeting

To hear others
please join audio

Join with computer audio
Test speaker and microphone

Roger Small appears, back to the camera, shuffling papers at the opposite end of the room. CUT TO: the head and shoulders of chairman Brian Tolver, the title 'Handforth PC Clerk' in the bottom left corner of his screen. CUT TO: each contributor in turn. (Note, if you prefer to read the meeting in GALLERY format, please click the icon. If your connection drops at any time, please try closing the book and opening it again.)

BRIAN TOLVER: When do we plan to start?

UNSEEN VOICE (whispering):   Fuck off.

JACKIE WEAVER: I think we could start at any moment, chairman. It might be helpful to go through the same things as before, which is to encourage people to switch off their microphones because it does reduce the background noise ... I'll continue to admit people if you'd like to start the meeting, chairman.

BRIAN TOLVER: Can we be assured we won't be thrown out of the meeting like we were last time?

JACKIE WEAVER: As long as we have reasonable behaviour from everyone, no one will be excluded.

BRIAN TOLVER: I was thrown out of the meeting; so was Councillor Burkhill.

PETER MOORE *(guitars and amps line the walls behind him) (leaning forward)*:   Quite rightly!

JACKIE WEAVER: As a point of order, chairman, could we start the meeting?

JOHN SMITH *(sitting in what looks like a damp cellar)*:   Chair.

*CUT TO: a black screen with the caption
'Julie's iPad' appears. CUT TO:*

BRIAN TOLVER: We haven't started the meeting yet.
Do you want to start anyway?

JOHN SMITH: Yes, I'd like to ask a point of order.

BRIAN TOLVER: We're not in a meeting so points of
order are not ...

JOHN SMITH *(peering into the screen)*: Has it started yet,
no?

BRIAN TOLVER: Points of order apply during the
debate and I want to ask Jackie, was it you who quoted
a point of order?

JACKIE WEAVER: Yes, it was indeed.

BRIAN TOLVER: Are you here as the proper officer?

JACKIE WEAVER: I am here offering support to
Handforth parish council in the conduct of this meeting this evening.

UNSEEN VOICE (muttering): You're not the proper
officer.

BRIAN TOLVER: Is that as clerk or proper officer?

JACKIE WEAVER: There's no difference between clerk
and proper officer.

BRIAN TOLVER: Of course there is. You must know
the basic law, I would have thought.

JACKIE WEAVER: Are we going to start this meeting?

BRIAN TOLVER: It isn't the role of someone who –
however kindly – volunteers to do the clerking for the

meeting, to act as the proper officer if they haven't so been properly appointed. That's against the law.

JACKIE is about to speak ...

... and let me also quote to you the orders of Handforth ...

JACKIE tries again ...

BRIAN TOLVER *(now really irritable)*:   ... will you *stop* talking!?
JACKIE WEAVER: ... unless we are prepared to ...
BRIAN TOLVER: Will you please listen?

JACKIE attempts to speak ...

... will you please listen? Will you stop being ... whatever it is you're trying to be ... and just clerk the meeting – if that's what you want to do.

JACKIE is once again steam-rollered ...

... points of order, according to our standing orders, are determined by the chair. If you want to raise a point of order as a councillor, you ask if you can raise a point of order, you state it and then the chair decides. It is not for the clerk to raise a point of order. It is not for the clerk to decide a point of order.

JACKIE is about to interject once more and . . .

. . . you must be aware of that; at least . . . God knows what you're doing in your job. if you're not.

JACKIE WEAVER: Shall we start this meeting or shall we elect an alternative chairman?

CYNTHIA SAMPSON *('Julie's iPad' is still a black screen but audio is connected)*: . . . it is. Oh, hiya. Yeah, I'm just in a meeting at the moment. Can I give you a call back when it finishes? All right. Bye . . . bye.

JACKIE WEAVER: So, chairman, albeit late, shall we get this meeting started?

The back of Councillor Barry Burkhill's head appears in what looks like a cupboard.

UNSEEN VOICE #1:   Can't see Jackie Weaver.
UNSEEN VOICE #2:   Who is this woman?
Julie's iPad *(indistinguishable gasping noises)*: . . .

CUT TO:

BRIAN TOLVER: We'll start the meeting and I want to repeat what I said at the beginning of the last meeting: that this meeting has not been called according to the law. The law has been broken.

JACKIE WEAVER: The meeting has been properly called . . .

BRIAN TOLVER: . . . will you please . . .

*Zoom focus switches to a screen captioned
'Aled's iPad'. Aled Brewerton sits next to
his father on a sofa. They are partly obscured,
their device's camera trained predominately
at the level of the pair's knees.*

ALED'S IPAD: Mrs Weaver, please!

JACKIE WEAVER: If you disrupt this meeting, I will have to remove you from it.

ALED'S IPAD: You can't!

BRIAN TOLVER: It's only the chairman who can remove people from a meeting. You have no authority here, Jackie Weaver – no authority at all!

Chairman Tolver disappears. CUT TO:

ALED BREWERTON: She just kicked him out. No, she's kicked him out.

ALED BREWERTON'S DAD: Don't.

ALED BREWERTON: She's kicked him out.

ALED BREWERTON'S DAD: Don't.

JACKIE WEAVER: This is a meeting called by two councillors ...

ALED'S IPAD: ... illegally ...

JACKIE WEAVER: ... you may now elect a chair.

ALED'S IPAD: No, they can't! Because the vice-chair's here. *I* take charge.

JACKIE about to talk, is interrupted.

... read the standing orders! READ THEM AND
UNDERSTAND THEM!

Silence ... gasps.

DAVID PINCOMBE: Dear me.

JACKIE WEAVER *(still in shock)*   Appalling behaviour.
A copy of this *will*, in fact, be sent to the monitoring
officer.

BARRY BURKHILL *(facing camera and angry)*:   Where's
the chairman? *(Further mutterings)* Where's the chairman
gone?

JACKIE WEAVER: ... like to elect a chairman for this
meeting.

BARRY BURKHILL: We don't have to elect a chairman. There's a chairman already installed. The chairman
of the council.

JACKIE WEAVER: Councillor Burkhill, we've been
through this.

BARRY BURKHILL: What are you talking about? You
don't know what you're talking about. *(Chuckling from
JOHN SMITH)* The chairman of the council is the ...
is the ... chairman of the ... of the ... council.

SUE MOORE *(head-only, framed by lavish
curtains)*:   Councillor Burkhill. Could I ask you to be
respectful to Jackie Weaver, please?

CUT TO: ALED'S IPAD. ALED BREWERTON'S
DAD rocks back and forth on his sofa, laughing.

JACKIE WEAVER: We can now elect a ...
ALED'S IPAD (off camera):   (Here comes the) subpoena
JACKIE WEAVER: ... chairman?

> *BARRY BURKHILL*
> *appears to have left the meeting.*

ALED'S IPAD: (*Mutterings*) She's kicked Barry out. No, Barry has gone. Shh ... (*strangulated noises*). We're trying to have a Teams meeting, you fool ... we're trying to have a Teams meeting, you fool ...

> *In the background, away from the screen in focus,*
> *are the sounds of suppressed rage and mad cackling.*
> *Cynthia Sampson now appears on 'Julie's iPad'.*

CYNTHIA SAMPSON: Jackie Weaver, I find that the person on Aled Brewerton's Zoom is being very disrespectful to everybody ...
ALED'S IPAD: Oh, coming from you, from Birkenhead, that sounds good.

> *'Aled's iPad' disappears from focus and from the*
> *line-up. He has been removed from the meeting.*

DAVID PINCOMBE: Thank God for that.

JACKIE WEAVER: We can now elect a chairman for the meeting.

SUE MOORE: Can I propose John Smith, please?

CYNTHIA SAMPSON: I'll second it.

JOHN SMITH: Thank you. My first point is to apologise to Jackie, but welcome to Handforth.

Pause.

May I start?

JACKIE WEAVER: Indeed. It's nothing if not lively in Handforth!

JOHN SMITH: Yes, well … what I would say is that it was a very good example of bullying within Cheshire East and the environs.

PETER MOORE *(now centred on-screen)*:   John, can I make a very quick point? It's rich coming from the chairman who hasn't held a meeting since March to try and call this one illegal. The man is a complete disgrace.

JOHN SMITH: OK, thank you, Peter. All right. I'll get started. Things to do: item one.

JACKIE WEAVER: Just before we move on, might it reassure the members of the public who are present that the meeting has been properly called? That, in fact, two councillors have called the meeting, which is quite proper and, because the Handforth chairman and fellow councillor joined the meeting, as a courtesy we allowed the chairman to take the chair. But now they have left, it is perfectly appropriate to re-elect a chairman for the meeting.

As the meeting continues, the odd noise drifts in, including the sound of a toilet flushing.

IAN BALL (*initially still muted*):   I noted before the chairman departed from the meeting, I noted that the label on his video said 'clerk of Handforth parish council'. Could anyone clarify how that came about and whether that is in fact the case right now?

JACKIE WEAVER: Yes, I did notice the moniker on the screen and it did make it quite difficult ... but, having followed this quite closely, the chairman simply declared himself clerk and notified everybody of the case and the remaining members have quite correctly refused to recognise that position but, as Councillor Smith says, I'm afraid there's no way of stopping him calling himself clerk. Please refer to me as Britney Spears from now on.

* * *

So, there you have it. The first few minutes of the Handforth Parish Council meeting in all its glory. We saw three very angry men try to dominate and derail a meeting with some time-honoured bullying tactics. They wouldn't let me or anyone speak, then disputed the legality of calling the meeting as well as my authority. After they had hurled a few extra insults, I removed them from the meeting. You see, as facilitator and host of the meeting, I *do* have the authority *and* I had a mute button.

Jackie Weaver tells it how it is

So, here's a little background to the meeting and how it evolved.

The start of the meeting

From the outset, we debated whether the meeting had started. The council meeting that preceded this one – the chairperson was removed that time, too – had begun in a similar fashion, with a general discussion about what time it was. I think most people agree that the time is well, the time, but in Handforth it is apparently dictated by the clock on Chairman Tolver's wall as opposed to the one on your computer screen.

I planned an orderly meeting and that meant suggesting everyone mute their microphones (mainly because you can clearly hear someone whispering 'Fuck off' at the beginning of the meeting. I could scarcely believe my ears on that one and had to replay the video at the end and yes, those words were anonymously hissed). It was clear that Chairman Tolver was still sore about the previous meeting and my response to him sounds like something a harassed mother or teacher would say to a troublesome group of children. At least he started calling me 'Jackie' after a bit, rather than always 'Jackie Weaver'.

Proper officer or clerk

The chairperson had demanded to know if I knew the law. Of course I do – I'm the chief officer of the Cheshire Association of Local Councils! But there was no point getting sucked into this side discussion and the best way to do that was to ignore Mr Tolver's patronising tone.

The clerk *is* the proper officer in almost every council in the country. Technically, the roles could be split but, in this instance, I knew the wrangling over definitions was more about picking a fight rather than getting to the bottom of legislation. I was acting as the clerk, which involves ensuring that the instructions of the council are carried out, and parachuting a clerk in to take a session is not that unusual. It's something I've done countless times. (Think of me as the Nanny McPhee of the parish council world – when they have a problem I'm there, and when they're running OK, I'm not).

Think of me as the Nanny McPhee of the parish council world.

I could have sent in someone else, but most of the councillors present knew me and had met me before (although they subsequently denied it). I thought that was a positive thing. I was aware of the specific issues Handforth had been experiencing over the previous couple of years. In effect, there had been two warring camps within the council and I thought, I'm going in myself. However, what I didn't realise was just how vitriolic it had become.

The interruptions

I knew within minutes or, maybe, seconds that the chairperson and his allies were intent on hijacking the meeting and shutting it down before it had started. So it proved. The chairperson delayed starting the meeting, would not let anyone raise a point of order and was clearly determined not to let me speak or respond to anything he said. He planned to put forward the proposal that the meeting was unlawful, knowing that he and his allies would outvote everyone else. The meeting would not have even started. I could see what he was up to and I was determined not to let that happen.

Julie's iPad

To be honest, the inadvertent humour of 'Julie's iPad' (otherwise known as Cynthia) was most welcome at this point, as she briefly stole the limelight from the verbal onslaught of Chairman Tolver when she forgot to switch her microphone off and we were all treated to her finishing off another call. I just couldn't believe how the chairman was behaving.

Was the meeting legal?

The meeting was most certainly legal. Usually, a clerk or, failing that, a chairperson calls a meeting, but the chairperson had unilaterally suspended the town clerk, decided to take on the role himself and had refused to call a meeting for some months. In this scenario, two councillors are empowered to call a meeting and, as they needed someone to help set it up and oversee it, they contacted my organisation.

The councillors who wanted the meeting to go ahead were and are passionate about Handforth – the local bus service, the neighbourhood plan, that kind of thing – and they were dismayed that the basic business of parish council life was not getting done. So, yes, the meeting was legal and I do understand the basic law (principally, since you ask, the Local Government Act 1972, which isn't perhaps a laugh-a-minute read, but it underpins everything we do in the world of parish councils).

In town council terms, the meeting you saw was an 'extraordinary meeting'. I remember, many years ago, I got terribly excited when I attended my first extraordinary town council meeting, hoping that it might actually have a few thrilling moments, but, alas, that wasn't to be the case. We don't mean extraordinary here in the sense of being 'great fun' – although Handforth's popularity might suggest otherwise – so much as it not being part of the ordinary schedule of monthly meetings.

The standing orders

Standing orders are the written rules of the council and regulate how meetings are set up and conducted. You might say they are our constitution. They are our bread and butter – I have read them and, yes, I bloody well do understand them. (I have hinted that I have the standing orders tattooed on places I wouldn't necessarily like to share.)

During the meeting, there were so many danger zones in terms of our discussions. None of them would advance the business of the evening. If I'd allowed myself to be dragged down into the standing order debate, then we would all have got lost. I needed to stay focused on what I had to do, which was to keep the meeting on track and not to let the really shouty men get to me.

The ejected councillors

Chairman Tolver, Aled Brewerton and his father and Barry Burkhill were all removed from the meeting because they were behaving unreasonably. In fact, I'd say their behaviour was shockingly bad, representing some of the worst examples of bullying and disrespect I have ever seen.

The three of them were like little schoolboys who had hatched a plan that had gone terribly wrong. I've seen the type before in council meetings: people who throw legislation at you, misquote rules, apply laws partially, interrupt you as you present information until – they hope – you get to a position where you can't remember if you're right or wrong or what the argument was in the first place.

No doubt these three assumed that I would be a bit of a soft touch. Would they have talked over me in that way and assumed I had no authority if I was a man? Well, they were intent on obstructing the meeting at any cost, but I'd still say probably not.

Even after they left, I reminded the remaining councillors that the disruptive members were still in the Zoom 'waiting room' area and I asked if the remaining participants wanted to allow them to return. Not surprisingly, the consensus decision was in the negative. Thereafter, the meeting continued, the remaining councillors covering many items on the agenda before setting a date for the next meeting, unaware that millions would eventually witness the extraordinary events of the Handforth parish council meeting.

Channelling my inner Britney

Just as Chairman Tolver decided to label himself 'Handforth PC clerk', I suggested that everyone refer to me as Britney Spears. I thought of someone who was as far away from me as you can imagine: young, blonde and sexy – but it served to highlight the point that, while I can call myself Britney Spears, it doesn't actually *make* me Britney Spears, just as calling yourself the council clerk doesn't magically grant you the responsibilities.

After the meeting went viral, another singer – Amy MacDonald, whom I mentioned I loved in an interview – sent me a signed CD. Yet Britney – who I'm told had more hits on her social media than she's had in a while, following Handforth – didn't so much as say 'Hello'. She might at least have sent a pair of her sparkly stage pants (I mean 'shorts' – please don't get the wrong idea here) . . .

Media sensation

Over a month after the meeting, a couple of students posted edited 'highlights' of it on YouTube and, overnight, I became a social media sensation, trending no. 1 on Twitter. Once I found out what that actually meant, I realised that, yes, my name and Handforth parish council were gaining a certain amount of notoriety beyond that of Cheshire East.

Suddenly, the media were at the door and I was asked to appear on TV and radio and to speak at political gatherings, universities and a variety of other events. Before I knew it, Piers Morgan claimed I was the greatest feminist icon since Emmeline Pankhurst, my face was appearing on fridge magnets and mugs, and I had been immortalised in sponge cake. And on top of all of that I got to meet (virtually, but that'll do) my screen hero, Anton Du Beke from *Strictly Come Dancing*. What a treat that was (for me, at least).

Why did the meeting go viral?

I think what people saw, and delighted in, was somebody taking a stand against the bullies in a very familiar, everyday environment, one to which people can relate and one that wasn't glossy or unreachably glamorous – by any stretch of the imagination. And in this ordinary scenario we saw karma – we saw some people doing the wrong thing and we saw consequences to their actions. We often hope for that kind of reckoning in life but rarely are we able to do it ourselves – and rarely do we see it played out before us.

And, of course, on some level it is extremely satisfying to watch people *totally* losing it.

Chapter Two

Meeting Etiquette: Dos and Don'ts

*If you have nothing more to do in your life than
attend meetings, you need a different life!*

Hosting or participating a meeting can be challenging –
especially if it includes people who seem to *live* for meetings or there's some kind of resentment, frustration or
hostility building in the room (virtual or otherwise).
Whether it's a high-level business meeting or the allotment
society AGM (which we all know can be particularly
brutal), passions can run high and disagreements break out.
And anyone who has sat in a rainy village hall staring at
item sixty-three on the agenda might also tell you that
meetings can also be, well, *boring*.

A big part of my job is to ensure that meetings are set up
and conducted effectively, that they achieve their objectives
and that participants feel able to contribute – without, for
example, someone screaming in their face that they have to

read the standing orders. Over the years, I have chaired and attended countless face-to-face and online meetings and can spot at a thousand yards the potential danger signs and how to nip in the bud any bubbling of trouble.

So, here are a few tips on holding effective meetings, principally those held online but many of the techniques could apply equally to those held in a council chamber or the back room of the local Dog and Duck.

Welcome!

Treat online meetings like physical ones. In a face-to-face meeting with a handful of people or more, somebody needs to steer or run the meeting, whether it's an appointed chairperson or the person who has called it. And that person should welcome participants to the meeting – in the case of online meetings, it might feel a bit odd welcoming people to their own home but it sets participants at ease and makes for a friendly atmosphere.

If there is no one steering the meeting, perhaps because the chairperson is unfamiliar with the interface, then the meeting can drift off course. And if the chairperson is uncomfortable with the technology? Well, they just need to get to grips with it or get someone to help.

The rules

It sounds obvious, but every meeting needs an agenda or, if it's a less formal event, a line or two outlining its purpose so everyone attending is on the same page.

If you've a lot to get through, set out some clear rules at the beginning of the meeting, make sure everyone is on board and keep it upbeat. In my world, meetings can be a little dull, so there's no harm in injecting a bit of humour or levity from the start.

I might start a meeting with something like:

Thank you so much for turning up – it's lovely to see you. It's been a really miserable morning, so I guess we've got nothing better to do. [Bit of a laugh – nice opener]

Right, we've got ten things to get through and it's important that I get you off on time because the rest of you have lives; it's only me who doesn't. [ha, ha]

If we go through these items in order – are we in agreement that we will give them five minutes each? If we need more time, we go into agreed overtime or we discuss them next week. Is everyone happy with that? [This builds in consensus as we go along and if Derek wants to talk about item four FOR EVER, then we can agree to leave that for next week]

Names and roles

Clarify or remind people of their roles and, in an online meeting, your name or some other *reasonable* moniker should be on the screen – we don't need your partner's name or 'Mike the Mechanic' or other such hilarity. You don't have to rename the device itself; you can just rename yourself in the meeting app and, again, if you don't know how to – find out! If agreed, switch your camera on and don't use a funny 'cat' or 'potato' face during the meeting. Remember – there is no one in the country that does not feel they know 'Julie's iPad'.

I know this has all been said before . . .

So, we get together for a variety of reasons but, in my experience, the purpose of most meetings is to make decisions and to inform people. Don't, whatever you do, have a meeting just for the sake of having a meeting or to facilitate those who like nothing more than the sound of their own voice (you know the type). If you have nothing more to do in your life than attend meetings, you need a different life.

Common to many meetings are the usual suspects who like to ask questions, which always brings to my mind that old saying, 'Some questions need to be asked and some just need to ask questions.' If they're not asking questions, these are the participants who prefer to make a lot of statements, starting off their two minutes' worth with 'I know this has all been said before . . .' Well, if it's all been said before, let's not say it again! Don't forget the chairperson of the meeting does have some power and, if you are beginning to feel tired and fractious, you can be sure others are too and will thank you for taking control.

Who would play me in a film?

I would choose Helen Mirren as I quite like her hair and maybe Richard Gere could be my husband Stuart – just pretend . . . of course!

Rethink the agenda

Online meetings can include a greater number of people than their in-person equivalents – that's certainly the case in the local council world, where we might have considerably more members of the public viewing meetings. Councillors are often deeply suspicious of people turning up who they don't know but we nonetheless need to embrace them (currently, in a Covid-secure way, of course)!

If you are reaching a bigger audience, you may need to revise your agenda accordingly. Where previously the more select groups of attendees might have been greatly animated by discussion of such topics as septic tank drainage and potholes, you might need to rethink what you talk about. Add something with potentially wider appeal, such as ideas for the new skateboard park, or shorten the meeting just so you keep the attention of your new audience.

Mute the mics

In an online meeting with a lot of people, it's usual practice that everyone should have their microphone muted unless they want to speak. The chairperson (or administrator) can also mute everybody and then release people, one at a time, to speak. There's nothing more distracting than hearing people talk to their children, pets or partners, finish off other calls or even, heaven forbid, flush the toilet in the background. And have you ever heard crisps scoffed out of the packet in front of a microphone? Not good.

Have you ever heard crisps scoffed out of the packet in front of a microphone? Not good.

Try not to interrupt others – unless you're not being given the chance to speak, and then you may need to. Maybe there's an option to use the chat facility of your app during a meeting, allowing you to send messages to individuals or the entire group – we don't always need to use our voices to make our points. In any meeting, you should aim to allow one person to speak at a time, and remember that, in an online meeting, there's often a bit of delay and you may need to wait a second or two for people to answer.

Listen

Meetings are forums in which people exchange information and views. Participants need to listen to each other properly. That might also involve something called 'active listening', whereby you not only listen to what people say but also take notice of their facial expression, vocal pitch, body language and even what they're *not* saying or the issues they move over quickly. You might also pick up on anyone who isn't contributing to a meeting perhaps because they feel uncomfortable or are being talked over (sound familiar?).

If you're having to write notes or minute the meeting, you can't actively listen or notice who isn't contributing. It might be helpful to have someone else take notes or perhaps record the meeting, if everyone's in agreement.

Auto-erotic texts

There's always the temptation to juggle other tasks when attending online meetings – especially if you're off-camera – and that might include sending a quick email, text or tweet. The problem is, it's easy to make mistakes if you're only half-focused on what you're doing – and you might be amazed at what auto-erotic prefects in scent massage (or, should I say, autocorrect can do to a perfectly innocent message). Before you know it, you might have told your manager that you're really hairy (hungry) or that you look forward to sleeping with them (seeing them). The horrific permutations are endless so always check that email, text or tweet before hitting send!

The location

If the only privacy you can get at home is in your bedroom, fair enough, but if you're lounging on your bed or settee with a computer on your stomach then you're not properly engaging with the meeting, perhaps?

For a work meeting, it's usually best for people to have a device each, otherwise you tend to get only half your head in the picture and the like. Also position the camera at roughly eye-level or higher – there really is no justification whatsoever in any Zoom meeting to have your nose-hairs on display.

Correct dress

Get properly dressed for an online meeting, and I don't mean from the waist up but all of you – it's all about an attitude of mind. If you're in pyjama bottoms, you're not really in your business head (although you might just about get away with slippers).

Pets

Don't have your pets on your lap during an online work meeting. I've had that a lot. Typical scenario: someone holds up their cat for everyone to admire, 'Oh, yes, it's lovely' (*another bleeding cat*) – and now I've forgotten what I was going to say ...

Food and drink

As in physical meetings, a drink, tea, coffee or whatever is fine but eating snacks is a bit of a no-no. I've seen people eating their dinner during an online meeting. Even if they have the sound off, it's still – well, unpleasant. And don't forget – people do notice how many times a wine glass is topped up, particularly if the meeting has only been going for an hour!

> People do notice how many times a wine glass is topped up, particularly if the meeting has only been going for an hour!

Own up to mistakes . . .

Council meetings, in particular, should be transparent. People need to see how decisions are taken. If things go wrong or you make a mistake, don't beat yourself up about it. I always say it's not the mistake that makes for a downfall, it's the mess you make trying to cover it up. I always own up to errors in meetings – which is probably why I would never make a good politician – and if you do the same, say what you're going to do to put them right.

. . . but don't repeat them

There's plenty of good practice out there that you can look up and follow in your own meetings *but* don't fall into the trap of thinking that if something works for somebody else then you should incorporate it into your life. You loved your colleague's virtual library background in a Zoom meeting and think the Bada Bing! club from *The Sopranos* would make the perfect background for you? Maybe not. Similarly, outside of work, those thick, black eyebrows might look fantastic on a few social influencers – although, honestly, the jury's out on that one – but are they really a good look for a retired accountant from Crewe?

Saying that about eyebrows, I should confess I have started pencilling in mine – just a little, and only because they're very fair and they don't show up on camera and that's where I'm looking at myself all the time. First thing in the morning, I say to my husband Stuart, 'Right, I've got my eyebrows on!' – and now it feels wrong if I haven't done them.

So, for an effective and well-run meeting, follow the rules and be considerate, as well as polite and open. Get comfortable with the technology, lighten up and, who knows, you might even make some good decisions and enjoy yourself, or at least get through those items on the agenda before *Game of Thrones* starts.

Meeting dos and don'ts

DO

Welcome people to the meeting

Have an agenda

Encourage *brief* introductions

Switch off your microphone when not talking

Listen

Dress appropriately

Own up to mistakes

DON'T

Give yourself a funny name or 'potato' face

Ask a million questions

Interrupt people

Slouch on your bed or settee

Have your pet on-screen or on your lap (so only the wafting tail shows)

Repeat the mistakes others make

Chapter Three

How to Get Things Done: Creating Order Out of Chaos

I'm sticking to my guns – this meeting is going to happen and nobody leaves until we've made a decision.

I have always liked to be in control because life was fairly chaotic when I was growing up. I was born in Motherwell in Lanarkshire, Scotland, where my father then worked at the Ravenscraig steelworks. From when I was aged nine, we moved several times because of his job, eventually heading across the border to England and settling in Alsager, Cheshire East.

Due to the various moves, I went to four different primary schools before I moved on to grammar school. Making friends was difficult when we were always on the move and those friends I did find were soon left behind. It was hard for me to open up and to this day I don't let many people in.

The relationship with my mother was also challenging. Her character was defined by what I call Scottish scratchiness and she was angry quite a lot of the time. This was no doubt exacerbated by health issues – problems with her stomach that meant she often couldn't eat and was in constant pain. The consequence for me was many days off school, looking after her. The doctors dismissed her out of hand, saying her illness was all in her mind, but I was there when her stomach ulcer perforated; you can imagine how frightening it was for me aged thirteen or fourteen to see my mum rushed to hospital. That, of course, proved that she hadn't imagined the whole thing, although it was only later that I was able to process what that must have been like for her.

The problems only increased when my mother got better and wanted to re-establish her position in the home. Until then I'd had to take on the role of mother to a large extent, looking after my younger brother, Billy, accompanying my father at various work events and cooking for the family. (I found out quite quickly that you can't put a frozen chicken complete with its plastic bag of giblets into a hot oven for an hour and pull out something tasty!) Now my mother wanted to reassert her role as matriarch and I felt a certain degree of resentment. It resulted in what I can now see was a power struggle. Sadly, I don't think we ever resolved our relationship.

There were so many unwritten rules when I was growing up. As an example, if my mother decided I needed physical discipline – a form of parenting that was all too common in those days – she'd come after me to give me a smack. I'd have to make it to the top of the stairs before her, knowing she would give up. I knew that if I didn't get there before her, I'd be in for it.

I lived in an unpredictable environment as a child, subject to my mother's moods and random aggression. It fed into that need I now have for order and rules and into my abiding desire for calm. I'm the kind of person who likes to get things done, even if bedlam is erupting all around me. And I know I'm not alone: there are women like me (and men, to be fair) up and down the country, who may not be the loudest or angriest people in the room, but they are the most effective. They get involved, get stuck in and, well, make things happen without making a whole lot of fuss.

Like me, this small army is probably happiest when there are a thousand different things that need doing – most of them seemingly impossible. I've certainly always kept myself busy whether it's at work, in my community or when bringing up my three sons. From running the local slimming club to facilitating parish council meetings, I like to think that things get done when I'm around.

Superwoman that I am (!), I do sometimes take on too much – at heart I know I'm a bit of a people-pleaser – but I've learned to recognise when that's happened and try as best I can not to repeat it. Here are some tips on how to control that ever-growing to-do list (although, believe me, I *love* a good list) so you too can create a bit of order in your life.

You can't do it all

Be realistic about what you can and can't achieve. It may look like some people have got it all covered but the reality is that they've given less priority to certain things in their lives. When

I'm busy doing my day job alongside various media interviews and the like, my darling husband Stuart will step up and take over household duties – shopping, cooking, cleaning, washing, the lot – it all just seems to get done by magic.

I'm able to let go of those things, even if it means we eat chips three nights in a row – which isn't great for my waistline, but needs must – because I'm not worried about those things being done 'my way' or to a particular standard. (Don't get me wrong, I'm not a total sloven, but you get my drift.)

Some things, however, I can't let go of, such as responding to correspondence. I do like to reply to emails promptly and I am known for my lightning-quick responses – I just can't abide having an email lolling about in an inbox unanswered. If you like to do a certain thing your way or to your high standards, you might as well do it yourself and let go of something else. It is no saving if someone else takes over some of your tasks and you simply fret over them.

Spinning plates

Even if you let go of certain aspects of your life, there may still be lots of other things pulling you in different directions; you can't give everything the same amount of attention all the time. Too many spinning plates means that something will come crashing down – that, or you'll simply run out of physical and emotional energy.

I combat this by visualising the different elements of my life – let's say they might comprise work, friends, children, self, etc – as boxes, each with a tight-fitting lid. When you are ready to open a box lid then make the conscious decision to do so. If you feel able to open two or three lids at once, then give it a go but should you start to feel overwhelmed emotionally or in terms of the time available to you, simply visualise one of the lids closing. In doing so, you're not ignoring or hiding from what needs to be done, but making a decision to deal with it later – when another lid is closed. You are still in control; it's just a different form of control, which helps to make order when your mind is in turmoil.

Lovely lists

I do like a meeting agenda and I do also love to make lists. I find that it helps me to keep in control and, as I write that list, I can take time to figure out my priorities. Personally, I love the physical process of writing the old-fashioned way, that feel of an ink pen on paper and the calming effect it has on me as the words flow.

A whole industry has sprung up around helping us to make lists alongside journaling – keeping a diary or a journal – which some people use to organise their thoughts and feelings. If a journal doesn't float your boat, it's not a problem – write your list on a sticky note, on your phone or create an elaborate Excel spreadsheet (there are also people out there who can't get enough of spreadsheets) – whatever works for you. Just taking the time to make that list can have a therapeutic effect and you can savour the moment when you tick off a task as 'done'.

My lists always include some quick wins – tasks that I know I can achieve fairly quickly or easily, scattered among the bigger jobs. You don't just need to start at the top of your list and work your way down.

My lists always include some quick wins scattered among the bigger jobs – tasks that I know I can achieve fairly quickly or easily, scattered among the bigger jobs. You don't just need to start at the top of your list and work your way down. And, yes, I'll procrastinate like everyone else, but only over a task that is not terribly important, and I'll carry it forward to the next day and get around to doing that more troublesome job when I'm finally fed up of seeing it on the list!

Be prepared

If I know I've got a busy or difficult day ahead, I'm a big fan of getting properly organised for what's coming up: checking I've got the relevant links for meetings or assembling what I need for the day ahead. I don't want to rush about in a panic before a meeting, nor do I want to arrive late just because I can't find the crucial bit of information I need. I know I would never catch up with myself and would be on the back foot all day. In the days before satnav (yes, they did exist), I remember I once found myself impossibly lost on my way to a meeting and was so late I sat in the car park till the meeting finished and went home. Had I been better prepared, I would at least have had time to look at a map!

Social media

Like most of us, I'm guilty of looking at my emails whenever they come in, but I usually manage not to get too distracted by them. If I am losing focus, I switch off notifications and perhaps look at them every couple of hours. When it comes to Twitter or social media, I scan through that first thing in the morning, perhaps after I've looked at the papers and there's something I want to comment on, but I'm not (as yet) addicted to that form of media, being fairly new to it.

Yet I do see how you can easily live your life virtually – social media, I'm learning, makes you feel both connected and disconnected from the world, connected in that you find out things are happening and people are talking about various issues, but at the same time it leaves you with this sense of, 'Oh God, there's only twenty-four hours in a day, how can I possibly keep up with everything?'

If I found myself scrolling through Twitter messages for hours on end, I might need to give myself a bit of a talking to. It all comes down to a bit of common sense – how am I going to get through that to-do list if I'm 'liking' a thousand posts on Instagram?

Stick to your guns

If you need to achieve something, perhaps when you're going into a meeting, try to remain clear and focused on your goal. If there are other, more assertive people, it's easy to get distracted or side-tracked and then all you do is talk about everything and resolve nothing.

In my work, I often deal with matters on behalf of other people, invariably for councillors who have called me in to resolve a certain issue. That helps to depersonalise the interactions; any disagreement or conflict that arises is not about me, it's about the ongoing issues.

Saying that, I can be pretty determined, particularly if I feel people aren't playing by the rules: this meeting is *going* to happen and nobody leaves the room until we make a decision. Otherwise, next time, I'll make sure we have so much background information circulated in advance we could drown in it.

Jackie's confessions

If I turn my mind to something, strange things can happen. For example, I have a bad back − incurred from having to move a bed when I was about fourteen years old (don't ask!) − and from time to time it can really incapacitate me.

Just like a number of women I know, I sometimes decide that furniture has to move, at which point strength will appear from nowhere. If I'm at home I'll move around all the furniture in a room, only then to put it back to where it was before, having convinced myself that it was all in the right place to begin with. If I get the urge at work, I can move a full filing cabinet and my colleagues in the office will ask in disbelief, 'You moved this?' And the bizarre thing is, if I went back to that furniture the following day, I wouldn't be able to move it for love nor money. The point is this: in the moment, when I decide that something has got to move, that's it, it has to move.

Just say no

If I'm honest, I'm not very good at saying, 'No,' to people − but I am getting better. If I like someone and they want me to do something, I'll say, 'Yes,' as I want to make them happy (it's that people-pleasing thing). But I will say no if I think they're taking advantage of me; I can be pragmatic with my commitments. If I've been asked to speak at a certain event for ten minutes, I'll do that happily, maybe stay on a bit afterwards out of politeness; but I won't hang about unnecessarily – I have learned to value my time: I'm a busy woman, lots to do, and, well, things to get done.

Getting things done

Pragmatism, focus and dogged determination are just some of the elements that help me get things done. I prioritise the things that are important to me and love to tick off those items on a to-do list, making sure I add a few quick wins along the way. And, talking of lists and quick wins, here's a lovely summary of points to remember:

You can't do it all – let go of some things

Stick to your guns

Make a to-do list and include 'quick wins'

Tackle items on that list one at a time

Get organised

Be focused

Don't waste your day on social media

Don't say 'Yes' to everything

Be kind to yourself!

Chapter Four

Dealing with Difficult People

Everyone has something likeable about
them – even if it's only their dog!

You may not be surprised to learn I don't like conflict. In fact, I would say I'm completely conflict-averse and I'll do whatever I can to avoid it. But there are times, of course, when situations and people spiral out of control – tempers rise, confusion builds and, before you know it, people storm off and refuse to listen to any kind of sense.

The bloodbath that we saw at Handforth was, of course, an extreme example, but sometimes people behave so badly that there's no quick fix solution to get them back on side. But there are a whole host of ways to deal with difficult people *before* you get to the door-slamming, screaming-at-the-computer-screen phase. And by difficult people, I mean those who are responsible for the different types of challenging behaviour we come across at work and in life

– from those who fail to see anyone else's opinion other than theirs to those who talk too little or way too much; from those who seem irritable, disorganised, or annoying in a way you can't quite put your finger on to those who are just downright rude every time you see them (OK, now I feel like I'm listing almost everyone I've met ...).

These people not only pop up with annoying frequency at work but every family has at least one difficult person in it – they are *everywhere*. There may be the odd example of the breed that you can avoid, but there are some – that one work colleague, the family member or even that tricky neighbour – who you have to deal with. Fortunately, there are ways and means to navigate this rather tricky process.

Look beyond the behaviour

I believe it is important to try to understand where a person is coming from in order to work out why they are being difficult. When someone is short or ill-tempered, our default is to think, that's just them – and, yes, sometimes that is true! BUT ... they could also have had a really bad day or their dog just died or any one of a hundred other things could be going on in that person's life. Listen to them, pick up on any visual clues that might indicate they're not sleeping well or similar, or ask around. And even if you don't find out what might be making them behave the way they are, accept there might be a reason for it.

Once you know or have a good idea why someone is being difficult, you're less likely to assume the problem is what they think of you and you'll be less likely to take it all personally, which then might stop things escalating still further. Try to remember that the world doesn't necessarily revolve around you; people have other things going on in their lives. Try to look past the issue between you. Who is the real person behind the story? Everyone has something likeable about them – even if it's only their dog!

Misunderstandings

Many of the rifts that arise in families or at work are the result of a breakdown in communication – people getting the wrong end of the stick and then stewing on it. We increasingly rely on emails, text and social media both at work and in our personal life and, let's face it, some people are really bad at written communication and that can feed into general misunderstandings or a rise in tension.

I remember at work having almost got to a point of complete breakdown in a professional relationship between my organisation and another. It got so bad I was getting emails from them on holiday and I thought, this is dreadful, there's no way we're going to be able to rectify things. When I got back from holiday, we tried a last ditch attempt to resolve the issue by meeting. We were some thirty seconds into our session together before we discovered that we had been looking at two completely different versions of a document and totally talking at cross purposes. When we could see that, the problem immediately disappeared. My advice? TALK to people, visit, pick up the phone – even the tone of your voice can convey so much more information than a text or email.

> **Talk to people, visit, pick up the phone – even the tone of your voice can convey so much more information than a text or email.**

Keyboard warriors

We've all come across them: people who are strident, aggressive, or breathtakingly rude in emails but as meek as can be when you meet them in person.

One person I know is so rude that every time an email comes through from them I can feel the hairs on the back of my neck standing up. And when they're being rude, they don't even use the 'shit sandwich' approach – you know, open and close with something pleasant, with the unpleasant bit in the middle. They're just rude and abrupt from beginning to end. And predictably, said keyboard warrior is far less hostile when you meet them in person, only brave enough to spew their venom from behind the safety of a screen.

During my fifteen minutes of fame, I was shocked by how many keyboard warriors out there felt they needed to share their thoughts on social media with me. What makes these people so angry and why do they take such umbrage at comments I make? And why follow me if you don't like what I say or stand for – even that I happen to be a woman? What I do know is that the problem is theirs not mine and I need to make sure I don't allow it to be mine.

So, how do we make sure we protect ourselves from them?

If you ever feel frightened or in danger, then do not hesitate to contact the police but if you feel OK and safe doing so, then challenge the behaviour. 'Would you say that – or how would you feel if someone said that – to your wife, mum or girlfriend?' Block them, report them to the platform moderators and, remember, they don't know you so their comments cannot be about you. Make sure you don't make them about you either.

People who go on and on (and on)

A Scottish friend of mine said of certain people, 'They make ma ears bleed': when someone talks too much we tend to switch off, not pay attention and sometimes that means their affliction becomes self-perpetuating. Perhaps they talk so much because no one ever listens to them. If you can break that cycle, by genuinely taking an interest and being sure to listen, it can be a real turning point for them. If the offending person is a work colleague, give them proper feedback: 'That's a really interesting point' or, 'I hadn't thought of it that way – tell me more' or, 'Why don't you put a report together for us to look at in the next meeting?' I once did that with someone I knew – I took time to listen to them properly and it made for an emotional experience for both of us as they no longer felt ignored or dismissed, and it touched me that such a small thing as listening could make such a big difference.

Jackie's confessions

One of the most difficult people in my life was my mother. She was domineering and we always had a strained relationship. Things came to a head when I got a boyfriend at the age of sixteen or seventeen. For some reason, my mum thought he wasn't right for me – even though he was a lovely lad, an engineering student. Or perhaps she thought I shouldn't be having a 'serious' relationship at that time in my life; it was never very clear. I think my mum had had a hard life: she was pregnant with me at nineteen and in those days you got married when that happened. My parents did just that and they stayed that way all their lives. I don't think they were entirely happy and I'm guessing my mother didn't want me to go down the same route.

Her behaviour throughout this time, though, was obsessive and I remember someone stopping me on the street once to ask if I knew that my mother was following me. I had no idea! She eventually gave me an ultimatum, 'It's either him or us.' Backed into a corner, I did what any teenage girl would do. I chose the boy and, not long after, on returning home from a night out, I found my bags on the doorstep.

I think I was still only seventeen at the time and I lived with my boyfriend and his parents until I got a job, then lodgings and eventually a flat in Crewe. Did we live happily ever after? Of course not. We lasted a couple of years and then drifted apart. My mother, however, stuck to her guns and we didn't have any contact at all for about four years. After bumping into each other one day in the street, we then saw each other from time to time, but never had what you would call a close relationship. Nor did we ever speak of the rift – it was as if it had never happened. When my father retired, they moved back to Scotland, which didn't help us maintain a relationship, and they have since both died. And I guess what I learned from that is that not everything can be fixed.

The quiet ones

There's often the assumption that everyone communicates in the same way or feels comfortable in a group situation or in front of a screen. Yet if you're with a bunch of friends having a coffee, there might be one person who is much quieter than the others; but they might be the one to give you a big hug when you leave – we all have different ways of expressing ourselves.

In meetings, some people are not comfortable vocalising their thoughts or ideas to a group of people. It might work better for them if they 'speak to a paper' by jotting down their ideas, which they can read or use as a prompt in a meeting or circulate beforehand and ask if anyone has questions. Perhaps they would like to email their points instead?

The disengaged

It might feel like you're banging your head against a wall if you're trying to get someone to engage or show a little bit of interest and you're getting nothing back in return (and if it's a young person, you might want to first check they aren't wearing Bluetooth earphones). But perhaps the problem might stem from the fact that they've tried and failed to get their point across and feel overlooked. Make a point of finding out and make it clear you value their contribution and give them credit for any input or feed-back they give.

It also doesn't hurt to look at yourself or the meeting itself – perhaps it is actually really tedious and it is more than flesh and blood can bear to stay engaged – or, in some instances, awake! Similarly, if people you live with are not natural talkers, then no amount of encouragement will help. Perhaps you need to learn their language and look at what they do rather than what they say?

Annoying calls

Some of the most difficult people we have to deal with are the scammers – and I'm thinking here of the people who call to inform you your tax code or bank account has been hacked or that your phone is about to be cut off unless you give them some personal information, etc.

That happened to me – for two weeks we had people calling my husband and me, threatening to cut off the phone if we didn't 'press 1'. Well, of course, being a savvy, switched-on pair, we did what I always suggest doing to scam callers: we put the phone down and got on with our day. That is, until our phone was actually cut off. It really had been the phone provider calling to tell us there had been a bit of a mix-up with the account. So, the message here is that sometimes it's really difficult to know when you are being scammed – it doesn't just happen to idiots!

Fallouts

Sometime relations break down between two factions or groups of people but in my line of work it's more common for individuals to do the falling out. People clash for all sorts of reasons: viewpoints, priorities or some kind of long-brewed resentment or personal history. Sometimes it's not even the history shared by the individuals but actually that of their families going back generations!

If there's a clash between other parties and all involved trust you, you can try employing mediation techniques yourself, such as talking to each person separately and giving them time to tell their story. If you can find some common ground, see if they are willing to talk together with you refereeing. If you manage them in a meeting, give them less opportunity to talk to each other directly.

If you are dealing with two warring groups, reaching a successful settlement is about getting people together and agreeing the terms of engagement – the rules they're going to play by. At Handforth, they didn't go down that route; perhaps the key takeaway, then, is to try to effect change before relations break down entirely. It might be worth getting someone a bit removed from the issue to act as an informal mediator as they might perhaps get some wider perspective on any disagreements.

Zero tolerance

There are occasions when you have to say, 'That is not acceptable,' if someone is overtly racist, sexist or abusive in a wider sense. Inappropriate language can be a real problem because it can easily cause offence and is hardly the best way to get people on your side. Of course, when emotions run high people can forget themselves, but nonetheless I don't think it's ever acceptable to have a fifty-year-old yelling 'f★★★★★★ idiot' in a meeting, however charged it gets.

Personally, I'd love to apply zero tolerance on certain forms of dress: I've known men attend physical meetings dressed for a campsite, wearing an outfit that might have fitted last year but is being stretched beyond endurance this season. I think men, in particular, refuse to believe their size changes. Believe me, trousers worn before the Covid-19 lockdown on a post-lockdown body may not be a good look!

Trousers worn before the Covid-19 lockdown on a post-lockdown body may not be a good look!

Subtle undermining

Anyone can be the subject of undermining and, just as is the case when it happens to a building, it can topple you. I had one situation in which there were two factions in a council, one of which was, shall we say, a bit rough and ready and the other a little more polished. The latter group would delight in subtly winding up the others and watching them go. They would rise to the bait every single time and the other group would say, 'See, this what we have to deal with!' In fact, the latter group actually started it and were the main culprits.

It's not easy to spot when you are being undermined – it is a subtle erosion in many ways, often targeting your confidence. Think of comments like, 'Oh, are you sure?' or, 'That's interesting' (before the speaker moves on to another topic) or, 'We don't really do it that way ...' It can seem perfectly innocent, while in reality the effect is of a gentle putdown that, over time, will have you doubting yourself. If you call out such interjections, you may hear, 'I was just trying to help.' I'm afraid the only thing that can help in this sort of situation is to develop an inner voice that you can use to shape your response and bolster your resolve. You know you are right, you have tested this to your satisfaction and that unhelpful input does not count.

My mother was an expert on the 'wee small voice' and was particularly skilled in the timing of its delivery. At my wedding, she helpfully told me – as I got into a limo on the way to the church – that it was brave of me to choose the dress I was wearing as I looked much less fat in the other one. What was the point of that particular comment? I couldn't run to the bridal shop and swap dresses – no, the point was to hurt and undermine. She always used to say, 'But I have to tell the truth.' I could never make her understand that sometimes there is an option to say nothing and that can work as well – an opinion is not always needed.

It's easy to be difficult

Difficult people come in all sorts of guises, from those who hide behind their keyboards or feel like they're never heard themselves, to the disengaged and the downright rude. Here's a quick checklist of how to deal with the difficult people in your life:

Try to figure out why they're being difficult

Talk to them, don't just rely on emails and texts

Listen to them and make them feel heard

Be alert to scammers but don't assume everyone is one!

Bring warring groups or individuals together

Don't accept overtly unreasonable behaviour

Develop your own powerful inner voice to drown out the underminers

Chapter Five

You Have the Authority: Women in Leadership

Alexa, does Jackie Weaver have authority here?
As long as there is reasonable behaviour, she has authority here.

I was told I had no authority. I, of course, did – as even Alexa will tell you – although the men who questioned my right to be in that meeting were convinced that they were in charge. They didn't like me challenging their authority and their response was to patronise me and to shout me down into submission. Would they have behaved in such a way had I been a man? I doubt it. But I do recognise that there are good men out there and that there are men who are subject to bullying too. No one owns bullying and we should all think about how we might stamp it out.

Nonetheless, in some quarters, there is still the age-old assumption that it is men who are running the show. While there are plenty of women who are in positions of authority across all walks of life, we still have a long way to go. As of July 2019, just 35 per cent of local councillors in the UK were women[*]. In the same year, women made up 50 per cent of those employed in Europe, but just 18 per cent of senior executives. As a result, women's views and life experiences are still under-represented at many levels of decision-making. No society can have a properly representative democracy if it does not offer the opportunity of hearing and delivering on a range of different perspectives.

As a result of inequality, many still equate authority with dominance and aggression, not helped by television giving airtime to the likes of Sir Alan Sugar, the irritable alpha-male who 'fires' his hopeless employees on a weekly basis. And this means, of course, that people – and this can apply to men and women – emulate this type of behaviour or otherwise think they lack the necessary traits to be effective leaders. We need to change the misconception of what a leader is and ignore the voices in our heads that might be holding us or others back. How do we do that?

Well, here's a few thoughts.

The meaning of authority

Some people might equate authority with being the loudest, most dominant person in the room. The person with

[*]https://www.fawcettsociety.org.uk/news/new-fawcett-data-reveals-that-womens-representation-in-local-government-at-a-standstill
https://www.catalyst.org/research/women-in-management/

authority makes decisions, gives orders and expects obedi-
ence from everyone else.

For me, however, that's not what authority is – not if you
want to influence people, lead by example or generate
respect. Authority, for me, is having a quiet confidence in
your position. An authoritative person doesn't have to exert
dominance at every opportunity. There may be occasions
when it is necessary to be the loudest, but this shouldn't be
a matter of course. The confident person does not need to
bend everyone else to their point of view.

Bad leaders

We've all come across ineffective leaders or bosses in our
time. In my world, and I'm talking chairpeople here, they
tend to fall into two camps . . .

1. Those who have been in the role for far too long.
They are never challenged and bring the meaning of the
word 'pontificate' into sharp relief. They start the meeting
and then on and on, sucking the energy out of the room.
Every agenda item has to have the view of the chairperson
first and, by the time the chairperson has finished, everybody has lost the will to live.

If someone says, 'Do you think we could . . .?' they'll
answer, 'No. We tried that fifty-five years ago and it didn't'
work.' So assured are they of their own position that they'll
happily drive everything with no one else on board.

2. Then there's the opposite kind: the type who are
really 'nice'; they want *everyone* to be happy and are not

content with the majority consensus. They need every person in a meeting to agree and if one person votes against them, they will focus on that one person. The problem is they want to be liked and they can't make a decision unless everyone is on board. They are making a classic mistake. Yes, we want people to be friendly at work, but we aren't necessarily all 'friends'.

Good leaders

A good leader is somewhere between the dictator/tyrant and the boss who wants to be everyone's friend. Again, this definition depends on what you think about authority and that's why some people in positions of power might come across as severe or uncaring. Women, in particular, might fear that if they show the feminine, nurturing side of themselves they'll appear more vulnerable. My feeling is that showing compassion for others, helping people and listening to, and remembering, what people say makes for the best kind of leader. Kindness is not a weakness.

To boldly lead . . .

I'm often asked if there are any leaders or people in authority I admire. I can't think of any real-life figures currently in the public eye – perhaps because our country seems to have a bunch of twelve-year-olds in charge. Instead, I'd turn to fictional characters on television or historical figures to find those I do admire; those who have the kind of traits we want from our leaders. Here's just a handful:

1 Captain Jean-Luc Picard (Patrick Stewart) in *Star Trek*. As captain of the starship USS *Enterprise*, he embodies everything I admire in an authority figure: he's powerful and in control but also caring of his staff and the opposite of Captain Kirk (William Shatner) who was far too emotional and easily distracted by 'the ladies' ...

2 Cersei Lannister (Lena Headey) in *Game of Thrones*. She's the most evil of this lot but she knows what she wants and, ultimately, I guess she does what she has to do to survive and to keep her family safe.

3 Mr Spock (Leonard Nimoy) in *Star Trek*. He's also in control, his actions are ruled by logic and he is almost entirely unsullied by emotion. He does have a softer side, although you have to watch quite a few episodes to see it.

4 Queen Elizabeth I of England. She was shrewd, determined and prepared to sacrifice her personal life for the greater good. Cate Blanchett as Elizabeth was also cracking in the film of the same name.

5 Edward Lewis (Richard Gere) in *Pretty Woman* – he's powerful, gorgeous but also needs rescuing.

The steps to becoming a leader

It might sound trite, but you need to believe in yourself if you want to become a leader, and if you don't, then you'll forever have what is known as 'imposter syndrome', that feeling that one day 'they'll' find out you're just not very good at what you do. And if you have that, you'll always need other people to tell you how well you're doing. And if other people forget to tell you that they think you're wonderful, then where are you going to get that personal reinforcement?

Similarly, if you're going to move up the ladder at work, head up a committee or take on some form of leadership, you need to put yourself out there, and not wait to be invited. You need to have confidence and belief in yourself and not solely rely on other people to give you that validation. Remind yourself of all that you've achieved, talk to a colleague at work to see if they could offer any help and let others know about your achievements. Your work won't always speak for itself and sometimes you need to highlight to others what you have done. People are busy and just as wrapped up in themselves as you are so you need to do what you can to stand out.

Sometimes I feel a bit of a matchmaker at work. We have a regular turnover of clerks in the area (which might not surprise you to learn by now) and if there's a vacancy, I might nudge someone to apply for it. 'Oh, I couldn't,' they might say. 'Yes, you could – just go for it.' And they do and they get the job and all they needed was a little nudge from someone whose opinion they trusted — it's just a shame they needed someone like me to give them the confidence to do so.

> # You need to have confidence and belief in yourself and not solely rely on other people to give you that validation. Remind yourself of all that you've achieved.

Jackie's confessions

I've been the chief officer of the Cheshire Association of Local Councils for twenty-three years and have worked with the association for twenty-five years overall. It's a much bigger organisation now than when it started. I've gained a lot of knowledge in that time and know my stuff when it comes to parish councils. In 2017, I also completed a three-year counselling degree at Derby University, where I did my placement focused on bereavement counselling.

When I first joined the association, I worked in a voluntary capacity and helped with general admin, including putting together the advertising for the role I do now. While doing that, I made a throwaway comment to the chairperson – although I also think I was testing the ground a bit – 'Do you know, I could do this job?' And he answered, 'Why don't you apply?' So I did, and I got the job.

Before I took on the role, I was a councillor for three years, although that wasn't really for me – it involved dealing with a lot of people and the public and wasn't my environment. What had prompted me to become a councillor? I had previously applied to be parish clerk, a role that was in the end handed to the chairperson's wife. This didn't seem fair at all to me and certainly wasn't in the rules. (And I'm a stickler for the rules.) I don't think I am alone in going on to be involved in local democracy because of wanting to address something I thought or felt was an injustice.

At school, I had originally wanted to study medicine – I loved the sciences – all those binary, right and wrong answers and rules! However, I had to support myself when I left home and, without the financial support from my parents, university wasn't an option. I did gain a place to study nursing but had to make a living until the course began so I found a job in computing and stayed for a while. Later I had a job at Mothercare before I married Stuart and went on to have our three boys.

Negative voices

To move up that ladder or take on more responsibilities, you need to believe in yourself and to stop
listening to the negative voice in your head that tells
you you're not up to the job. Your voice might take the
form of the critical parent you can't quite shake off in
your mind or that partner who has a tendency to belit-
tle you – it's personal to you. But you can change what
the voice says or make a positive choice to stop listening to it.

Try not to zone in on the negative or put yourself down
as soon as you meet people. 'Sorry about that spot on my
face – it's dreadful, isn't it?' Would they even notice if you
don't mention it? And don't apologise every three seconds!
'Sorry' is a really important word but we shouldn't need to
use it often.

Similarly, there may be people who have a negative
influence on your life – if you can, stop seeing them! You
might also have had people around you who have been
really supportive and said encouraging things, but you've
decided to edit them out and only focus on the negative
comments – it's something we all do. Try focusing on the
good things and enjoy any compliments that come your
way.

Fifty-fifty

Women often expect too much of themselves. I was chat-
ting with the mayor of Bath recently (as you do) about the

way that a woman looks at a job description. She and I agreed that if a woman thinks she can do 50 per cent of the job, she often won't apply for the role because she'll also be thinking about the 50 per cent she can't do. A man, however, would think that 50 per cent was enough and would go for the job. That needs to change! And yet, it's not something that can be changed from the outside. Only you have the power to do this for yourself.

Confidence

You can't have confidence or speak with authority if you haven't got a clue what you're talking about. For that reason, you need to work hard and do your homework. In my line of business, we have laws for local government and standing orders – which I have read and understood, really well, as it happens – and that gives me the confidence and authority to do my job.

This doesn't just apply to local government; much of what we do in life comes with standing orders – by which I mean accepted rules and regulations – and before you can be an authority on anything, you need to understand what the rules are. Prepare for meetings, do some background research, know your stuff and if someone throws a curveball or something goes wrong, you'll be better positioned to handle the issue.

Winging it

There are times when we have to improvise as we go along – heaven knows, I seem to do it regularly these days! We can't always be expected to know everything and if you are asked something and you don't know the answer, be honest. When it comes to local government, I should really know the answer, but if I'm asked a random question in a media interview about, say, the state of the NHS, I'll express a view, but I won't present myself as an 'authority' on it. (Note to self: never become a politician.)

Quiet confidence

Authority is not about throwing your weight about and shouting the loudest. It's leading with quiet confidence, knowing your stuff and showing some kindness when it's needed. Think about leaders or bosses you admire; you might just have what it takes to become one of them. Here's a quick summary of how to get there.

Believe in yourself and don't solely rely on validation from others

Put yourself out there and shout about your achievements

Don't try to please or befriend everybody

Stop listening to those negative voices around you and in your head

Do your homework and gain knowledge

Be honest when you don't know something

Don't pretend to be an 'authority' on something when you're not!

Chapter Six

Be Assertive. Be Heard. Be Human.

Would you *listen to you?*

What does assertive mean to you? I know what it means to me, but you might think of something different. I'll tell you what it is not, and that's shouting. If you want to throw your weight about or just make a noise then by all means shout. But if you're trying to engage with someone, get a message across, persuade others to change their mind or make yourself heard, shouting is not the best approach.

The point is that the louder you shout, the less people listen. When you are shouting, you are no longer in control of your words (or your brain for that matter) and you are no longer listening. And if you go really ballistic – screaming something like, I don't know, 'READ THE STANDING ORDERS!' it can become almost farcical, prompting other people to laugh out of shock and embarrassment (mainly for you).

There are, of course, other, less confrontational ways you can be assertive, be heard and be human – by which I mean being a decent human being. But to begin with, have a good look at yourself – there may be a reason why you're never heard ...

Don't be dull ...

Is there a reason why no one seems to listen to you? Would *you* listen to you? Do you tend to bring everyone down the minute you walk into a room? Do you whinge on about socks, the bus timetable, that stubborn stain on the carpet all day? Are you the type that never has a good word to say about anything or anyone from the minute you wake up to when you go to bed at night? And if so, can we really blame people if they switch off once you get going?

You need to change the record. Yes, you might be having a bad day, a bad week or even a bad year but lighten up, say something positive (or interesting), compliment someone, make a joke. If anything, it'll make you feel better and others around might actually tune in to what you're saying.

... or vague

Be clear in your mind what you are trying to say or achieve, because if it's not clear in your head, how will you convey what you want to someone else? If you're in a relationship, you're unhappy and want it to be better, what specifically would make it better? If you don't know, then how will your partner know? Similarly, if someone at work has upset you, figure out what it is they have done to upset you and tell them what it is.

Don't be non-specific and expect people to read your mind – some people (*ahem*, my husband for example) are not very good at reading those emotional signals and need clarity. Others are just busy, with a ton of things competing for space in their heads, and they sometimes haven't got time to figure out what's going on in your head. Phrases like 'I need you to be more supportive' sound good but what is it you are actually asking for? Do you want help putting the children to bed or a night off, or do you just want someone to sit and listen to you?

Be clear and get to the point. Don't tell them what you *don't* want or like – tell them what you want in a positive way. 'It would be great if . . .' or, 'I would like it if you would pick up the kids on Saturdays/spend the evening with me/deal with that client for me,' etc.

Do you whinge on about socks, the bus timetable, that stubborn stain on the carpet all day?

I may be wrong but . . .

Some people – mostly women, I find – have a habit of putting themselves down or almost apologising before they say something, which doesn't exactly sell what they're about to say. They say, 'You're not going to like it, but . . .'

SO WHY SAY IT?!

If you want to be assertive and heard, don't frame what you say with negativity but take responsibility for what's coming out of your mouth: 'This *is* what I think and I think you're going to like it.'

I'm just putting this out there

Another pet hate of mine are people who say something, then immediately negate what they've uttered. This technique is often employed by those who haven't considered what they are going to say but are determined that they're going to say it anyway and let you deal with it. Either that, or it's a way of offering an opinion when it's not really wanted. My mother was very good at that – she always had an opinion and would feel compelled 'to just put it out there' – however cruel it might be. I could never make her understand that sometimes you could say nothing and that would work just as well – probably even better.

A wall of words

The way you speak obviously influences whether your audience can, or wants to, listen to what you're saying.

You need to come across as, well, a nice normal human being, and not someone who looks down at their notes or feet the whole time, or who mumbles or fails to interact with their audience in any way. Similarly, if you speak really s-l-o-w-l-y and everything you say is very flat and monotonous, the chances are that people will switch off; they'll lose interest, start to think about what they're having for dinner that evening or turn their attention to their phones.

There are also those people who, when speaking, hit you with what feels like a wall of words. It can sometimes feel like an almost physical experience. They wash over you – words, more words and still more words; no time to digest anything; you feel pressured to keep up and the only way to protect yourself is to stop listening.

If it's you doing the talking, perhaps you're giving a pres-entation, vary the tone and speed of your voice to keep people engaged. Don't attack everything with the same vigour or express wild enthusiasm about *everything* because the audience won't have the energy to keep up and they, too, will switch off.

Pick your battles

If you are determined to speak for three minutes on every item of the meeting agenda, people will be so sick of your voice by item fifteen that they will have tuned out. And, surely, you're not really interested in every single point? Can you really be passionate about everything? Usually

– and we can assume this is the case with most meetings – there will be things that you really care about, some that you're maybe a bit interested in and other items you don't give a monkey's about. Let someone else talk about the latter – they might actually care.

Always try to avoid heading into a meeting or starting up a difficult conversation if you're feeling very emotional or angry about something. If something has upset me then I might not talk it over with my husband Stuart for a couple of days; I don't want to relive the experience straight away and sometimes I need to process events on my own before I'm ready to start the conversation.

Jackie's confessions

I have a really happy marriage, but I have learned to accept that Stuart and I communicate in different ways, as is common whenever men and women talk to each other.

If I was meeting up with a female friend, perhaps someone I hadn't seen for a while and I said, 'Talk to me' or, 'What's going on with you?' etc., she might answer, 'I've been thinking about my mum and how she's getting on' (i.e., she's a bit worried) or, 'I've been looking forward to my birthday party' (i.e., she's in a good mood); conversational elements that give me some indication of her emotional state.

Ask Stuart the same question and invariably you'll get something like, 'I went to the tidy tip on Friday and it was really busy.' He communicates a fact with no insight into what's going on in his mind or how he's feeling. That's your lot.

In a similar way, if a woman comes home after a difficult day and wants to talk about it, sometimes they don't need their partner to 'fix' the problem. They just want their other half to listen: they want to be heard. They might not need a practical solution or to have an explanation of why someone was giving them grief, they just want a bit of sympathy – and perhaps a nice glass of wine (or a chocolate Hobnob).

Show what you mean

Some people are good with words, while others prefer to convey their meaning with pictures. Some grasp a concept better if they're shown an image. Drawing a picture or diagram or showing a film could get across the sense of your idea or perspective more effectively than by just talking about it.

In the same way in personal relationships, some people are better at showing their affection or expressing themselves through what they *do* rather than what they say. If this is your partner, they might show they care by making you a cup of coffee or folding the washing, small things that sometimes get the message across better than words.

Jackie's confessions

If I'm asked who I might consider to be my real-life heroes – as in, thoroughly decent people who were in their own way assertive or knew what they wanted in life – only two people come to mind:

My dad, because he was the most ethical person I've ever known. He was strong, forthright, proud of the men he managed at his steelworks and fiercely protective of them, and he very much believed in leading by example.

My gran (my dad's mum). She was the kindest person and she saw good in everyone, no matter how hard it might be!

The wrong audience

If you're struggling to make yourself heard, ask yourself if you're attempting to influence the right audience. There's no point putting forward a passionate case for the creation of allotments in your local area if you're speaking to the committee responsible for public transport or planning. Likewise, if your partner is not listening to you, despite everything you try, maybe he or she is not the one for you. Or could it be that they are experiencing difficulties themselves that make it impossible for them to take on board your worries or concerns?

Similarly, if you can't get heard, think about the people you're trying to engage with – what's going in their world? Are they strapped for cash, overloaded with work and unable to take on your new and exciting ideas right now?

Super-powers

If I could have one Marvel-like ability, it would have to be invisibility. I'd really enjoy being able to listen and watch people without having to interact with them. Imagine going into places that we don't usually get access to – maybe a prison or behind the scenes at a concert – *and* I wouldn't have to dress up or put my 'face' on!

Say 'No'

Don't say 'Yes' to everything because you don't want to let people down or it feels too awkward to say 'No'. Put yourself first sometimes! I know it can be difficult and I've certainly said 'Yes' to things far too often and then lived to regret it.

What I have learned is that when you say, 'No,' try not to go into lengthy explanations why you can't do something as you'll end up tying yourself into knots. There are persistent people out there, such as the chairperson of your local PTA who, before you know it, will have you heading up the school fun run, either because (A) you were too slow to say, 'No' or (B) you could only come up with a flim-flam excuse for getting out of it.

When you say 'No,' be firm, succinct but also polite: 'Sorry, no' or, 'No, afraid I won't be able to' and leave it at that. DO NOT add, 'I have an online yoga class' or, 'I would love to but I can't find a babysitter that night,' because that pushy chairperson will convince you that the yoga class can wait or she'll find a babysitter for you and you'll have no choice but to head off to that committee meeting when you'd much rather be doing the downward dog in your front room.

If you've been close to saying 'No' and convinced yourself to go because it just might be the best night of your life . . . trust me, it never is.

Engage, don't rage

Don't shout or lose your temper. If you want to be heard and get your point across in an assertive way you need to engage with people and make them feel like you're on their side. They're more likely to do what you want. Think about how you come across. Do you ramble on about the same old stuff? When you speak, does it sound like you're reading a shopping list? Is your audience inspired by what you have to say? Take responsibility for your own thoughts and words, think clearly about what you want and when you say, 'No,' mean it. If you want to stay in, eat Maltesers and watch *Pretty Woman* for the twenty-fifth time instead, then do it.

Be clear in your own mind about what you want

Think about what you're saying and how you say it

Don't ever start with 'I may be wrong' or, 'I'm just putting it out there'

Vary your tone, intonation and enthusiasm when speaking

Don't start an important meeting or conversation if you're angry or upset

Make sure you're speaking to the right people

Remember that images or action may work better than words

Say 'No' politely and succinctly

Be a nice human being

Chapter Seven

Keep Calm and Press Mute On the Noise

*What's the worst that could happen? They're
not going to take you out and flog you.*

Many people equate stress with a busy schedule but the
most stressful thing in the world for me is an empty diary.
Some might think, oh great, that'll give me time to do all
those things I've been meaning to do. Not me: I like my
work and I love to find solutions for things that aren't
working properly. I can feel almost paralysed if there's a
great expanse of nothing ahead. And if I don't work, I feel
I don't deserve time off – I guess it's that Scottish work
ethic coming through. We Scots are a tough breed.

The key is to identify what level of stress makes you
comfortable and at which point you no longer feel calm or
in control. It's true for me that, while I like to be busy, I do
sometimes take on too much and there can come a time
when I can no longer find a way of digging myself out of

the piles of stuff coming down on top of me. I may not see it coming, but I know when I'm starting to feel over-whelmed. At that point, I do try to cut down the schedule a little to make some more space for myself.

Over the years, I've learned various ways to keep calm and in control. I still get as irritated as hell by some things – and there is one particular thing that sends me into a blind panic (I'll reveal all later in this chapter) – but I also have a few go-to activities at home that help me to unwind and press mute on all that noise . . .

And another thing

We all have to deal with trying situations in life and it's often those difficult conversations with work colleagues, family or friends that can really test our patience and ability to keep calm. At work, I try to focus on what I want to achieve, so that if I get flustered, I know where my base is, even if others are trying to take me in a different direction. By clearly stating one point or objective, rather than trying to cover a lot of ground, you'll be able to keep people onside and head off opposition.

Sometimes, I'll use this kind of approach away from work. Recently, I had to have a difficult conversation with one of my sons. We had tried to talk things out but this had ended with me meeting a wall of silence from him, in turn triggering shouting from me; I really needed a Plan B if we were going to make any headway. So, when we next talked, I tried to keep focused on the one thing I wanted to achieve, to avoid having the conversation stray into other areas or escalate into another almighty blow-out. (If you find yourself saying 'and another thing . . .' during an argument with a family member, you may have lost some of that focus or composure!)

> If you find yourself saying 'and another thing . . .' during an argument with a family member, that's a sign you may have lost some of that focus or composure.

Both barrels

To get what you want out of any situation, you need to stay calm. If you decide to head into a meeting (family or business) and hit people with both barrels, head-on, first thing – that may work, but what if it doesn't? Where are you going to go from there? There really isn't anywhere else for you to go other than to continue to do more of it – and will you achieve what you want or have a reasonable conversation about a particular issue? Probably not.

Signs of stress

Do you keep putting on your underwear inside out? Or put your car keys in the fridge? Or miss a turning on a regular journey or find yourself driving through traffic lights when they're red? Don't ignore some of the little signs that might indicate that you're perhaps dealing with too much.

Distract yourself

We all have to do things that make us feel uncomfortable and for me that means going to the dentist. To get through it, I use the time-honoured approach of distraction. We do this with our children, but don't forget it works on adults too. If I'm sat in the waiting room, I might study the wallpaper on the wall: how many times does the pattern repeat? Why on earth did they choose that colour? Which strips aren't quite matching? Or I might strike up a conversation with the receptionist – how long have you worked here? Or, Where do you live? And while my brain is working on the questions and hearing the answers it has less time to think about what's making me anxious.

Take control

Feeling like you're trapped can also induce panic but, in most situations, you are not physically a prisoner. You can usually tell yourself that you can leave at any point and that you can make it your choice to remain – this is something

I tell myself at the dentist. It's a powerful statement and makes me feel more in control.

When I was giving birth to the last of my sons, I agreed to have a caesarean under epidural anaesthetic, meaning I would be awake during the procedure. It seemed like a good idea at the time but, as the eleventh hour approached, I was beyond frightened. I got through it by taking it minute by minute: I will do this for one more minute and then if I'm unhappy, we'll stop and I'll ask for a general anaesthetic. Saying that to myself helped me to feel like I had some control and get through the experience. That said – I haven't been back for another!

Pet peeves

I may seem supremely calm, but certain things do irritate me (I am human after all) . . .

1 Wimp behind the wheel

I don't get aggressive behind the wheel of a car – unlike some, who seem to get very fired up, honking at every minor infraction they encounter. Who appointed them guardians of the highway, anyway? Saying that, I might drive a little faster if I'm agitated, prompting my husband to ask, 'Are we in a hurry?' And, admittedly, I often haven't even noticed I'm doing it.

In general, however, it's not other drivers who irritate me, it's myself as I can't – for the life of me – master the art of overtaking. Where I live, we have narrow roads and few overtaking opportunities but we do have lots of slow farm vehicles and yet I'm useless at overtaking them – it drives me potty. I need to have fourteen miles' clearance on a straight road before I feel comfortable in taking the lead. And what annoys the hell out of me the most is when the car behind overtakes me *and* the car in front and I'm still stuck there, driving at ten miles an hour.

2 Friendly dog owners

I have two West Highland terriers – Westies – Izzy and Rosie. I loved the idea of having 'second-hand' dogs and contacted the Westie Rescue Group. They advised that rescue Westies generally don't make good family or lap-dogs because they can be a little bad-tempered so we got them as puppies instead. Izzy and Rosie may be small but they are very powerful for their size and really protective of us. Living where we are, in a rural setting, they are quite nervous of other dogs and people as they do not come into contact with many strangers. Izzy also does not like small people – I don't just mean people under five-feet-two but children – she gets very anxious when they're around and she can be a little 'bitey' if she feels threatened.

What tends to happen, unfortunately, is people just go ahead and make the assumption that the dogs want to be petted and that it's OK if their own dog wants to make friends. Neither belief is true. I do my best to keep our Westies away from people and dogs they don't know, but those other owners are all too often determined to come and find us. Go away!

3 Poo bags

Staying with the dog theme, everybody uses them and they are another one of my pet hates. I'm talking poo bags. Yes, by all means use them if you live in a built-up area but if you live somewhere rural like me: why are you putting your dog's doings in a bag? And then flinging it in the hedge? Just put it under a hedge, stone or bush where no child will step on it – much better for the environment – and who wants to see thousands of those horrible little bags everywhere? If they were intended to be hedgerow decorations they would come in assorted colours.

The world will not end

When something goes wrong, people often say things couldn't be any worse. But, invariably, they *could* always be worse! People love to catastrophise events and, at work, I sometimes come across colleagues who might be having sleepless nights about a particular problem. I get them to think, What's the worst that will happen? You're not going to be taken out and flogged, are you (well, at least in our sector, you're not)?

When I was younger – and, yes, I do remember being young – I too was probably guilty of excessive worrying, especially about embarrassing events. If my skirt was tucked into my knickers leaving a room, well, I would think the world had noticed and my life was over. The reality was that the whole world did *not* notice. There comes a point in life when you gain a bit of perspective and realise that things might be awkward but life goes on.

Head case

More recently, something rather embarrassing did happen. On leaving a meeting at work – a face-to-face one, remember those pre-pandemic happenings? – I realised that I had some bits of toilet paper stuck to my forehead, as I had wiped my face with some tissue before going into the meeting. As a younger person I probably would never have gone out in public again ... But, now? Well, it just makes for a funny story.

Jackie's confessions

I'm pretty level-headed and rarely get flustered but there is one thing that sends me into a total panic and over which I seemingly have no control. I guess you could say it's a phobia: I have a physical reaction, as if my brain has detached from my body. And this feeling is much stronger than dislike; I don't like heights, but if needs be I can take myself to the edge of a tall thing and look over.

So, what is the one thing that terrifies me, Jackie Weaver, chief officer and slayer of local council demons? Well, it's frogs ...

I think it all started when I was around eight years old; my family and I were in the north of Scotland and had driven to a loch for a walk. After we parked up, I jumped out of the car and started running down the wooded pathway towards the water. Halfway down that path, I suddenly realised there were frogs *everywhere* – it must have been some kind of mass migration because the pathway was literally teeming with them. I was frozen to the spot, paralysed by fear, as frogs crawled and leaped all around me (other than a few closest to me that were squished) and, all the while, my parents and brother were wetting themselves laughing.

Ever since, the sight – or even sound – of frogs has sent me into something of a spin. I have tried to overcome the fear, as the logical part of my brain tells me that I should be able to conquer it.

Not so long ago, we had a frog in the greenhouse and I thought, come on, Jackie, you can do this: get your big girl pants on. I got hold of the children's old fishing net on a cane and, just to be extra careful, fastened it to another cane so it was about twelve feet long. That meant I could stand outside the greenhouse, while I guided the net towards the frog. So far so good – but then it moved. The scream that ensued was completely involuntary (I never scream) and, now in full on manic response mode, I tried to get both my feet off the ground in a sort of crazed stepping motion. The result: the frog stayed in the greenhouse.

There was another incident at the farmhouse where we lived. From the dining room – yes, I know, we're posh and have a dining room – I was sure I could hear the sound of frogs. Stuart couldn't and assured me I was hearing things,. A day or so later, we were sat in the living room and bugger me if a frog didn't hop across the floor.

Stuart discovered that the cellar underneath the dining room was not only full of water but also full of frogs – all of which were eventually fished out by my sister-in-law (who, as luck would have it, was in the process of building a pond). I had at least discovered that I wasn't going completely ga-ga although the cellar thereafter was a complete no-go zone.

Keep things light

I often find humour helps to diffuse a tense situation. Sometimes, at work, I'll add in something jokey and other times I don't notice I'm doing it or, I confess, I just can't help myself. There are times when something is begging to be said – and I can't not say it ('Call me Britney' might be one of those instances).

I also do a lot of training in what is a very dull subject (local council law and procedures). By about two in the afternoon, I can see people are flagging and I find injecting a bit of humour keeps people with me and their energy up.

It also helps them to remember the twists and turns of the Local Government Act 1972. So, if we're discussing 'Decisions are taken by a majority of those present and voting', I might paraphrase that with something like, it's all about 'bums on seats', etc.

Down time

Here's what I do when I'm not battling it out in a parish council meeting. I find these activities relaxing and they make a good antidote to a demanding day.

1 I play games like Tetris or Solitaire. They're repetitive and take up just enough of my attention that my mind isn't able to focus on anything else. I don't like playing games with anybody else. I'm horribly competitive, can't cope with losing and I have even been known to cry with frustration, particularly during a game of Monopoly or Cluedo.

2 I love to paint my nails and have been doing it for forty-odd years. I'll carefully choose what colours and patterns go together and I'm pretty good at doing it. I have, in the past, had them done in a beauty parlour but I would go away thinking that I could have done a better job.

3 I love a good horror movie. In fact, I like nothing better than a good apocalypse. I think they are fascinating. I love to watch the collapse of society and see how people react. I also like to watch those really awful films in which annoying American teenagers die horribly – you know the kind; characters chased through the woods and terrible things happen to each of them. Don't get me wrong, I don't like seeing cruelty, torture or long, drawn-out deaths – I'm definitely not into realism here – but I'm fine with a bit of blood and guts, that kind of thing.

Saying that, I don't like too much suspense in films – it gives me a headache. I like to know how things will end and will watch the end of movies first or check out the synopsis on IMDB.com as I don't want to invest any emotional energy in characters who get killed off early. Doesn't everybody do that?

4 I do also read a bit; naturally lots of horror writers, such as James Herbert, Stephen King, Mervyn Peake, that kind of author. And, as with the films I watch, I'll read the final pages first so I know who's left at the end. I also read a lot of self-help books, like *Fat Is A Feminist Issue, Men Are from Mars* ... or *The Victim Triangle* – I guess I'm always trying to understand people a bit better.

I find injecting a bit of humour keeps people with me and their energy up. It also helps them to remember the twists and turns of the Local Government Act 1972.

Calm and healthy

So, there you have a smorgasbord of various ways to keep calm and maintain a healthy perspective in all sorts of potentially stressful situations, along with some insight into my likes and dislikes and things that can irritate or delight me. If we could merge them all into some kind of horror movie – American teenagers being splattered by poo bags or ravaged by over-friendly dogs – now *that* would make for a fun night in ... or maybe that's a bit Kafkaesque? Just don't show me a picture of a frog.

Don't let arguments escalate, focus on your objective

Don't go into a meeting with all guns blazing

Spot the signs when you've taken on too much

Distract yourself (or others) in uncomfortable situations

Tell yourself you're in control and at any time you can leave the situation

Things are never as embarrassing as you think

Don't take everything so seriously – draw out some humour

Have some down time and find activities that help you to wind down

Chapter Eight

Dealing with Adversity (and Loss)

I have no wish to live in a post-apocalyptic world – who wants to live on a planet where you can't shop?

Things go wrong in life. That's a fact. You might be sailing along pretty well, no major grumbles until, BAM, you're hit with something that stops you in your tracks. Totally unexpected, out of the blue and, suddenly, your day – or life, even – is veering off in an entirely different direction.

While TV and media might lead us to believe that life has a plan, that we'll always triumph and have a happy ending, the reality is that things do not always go as we hope. And thinking there is some sort of universal karma at work that will deliver our just deserts will only lead to disappointment. The setbacks that we face can range from those everyday mishaps – from getting a flat tyre to the internet going down – to more serious challenges, which might encompass losing a loved one or your job or your children leaving home.

We can't stop these setbacks happening – although, if it's your computer, you might try switching it off and on again – but we can arm ourselves more efficiently to deal with their effects. Your misfortunes may be truly awful but the vast majority of difficulties we face in life are minor bumps on the road – they might set you off course, stress you out and dent your bodywork a bit, but you keep on going. It's how you recover from those incidents that counts. It is important to live in the moment *but* it is also really important to take time to look at the bigger picture – only by doing that can we put these trials and tribulations into context.

Car escapades

When I think about the various mishaps in my life, it's amazing how many of them seem to be related to cars. And I'm not even a bad driver – I've driven tractors, I'll have you know – and I'm often the driver in our house. Nonetheless, here are a few incidents and thoughts that might strike a chord with fellow car-owners.

Where did I park my car again?

There's a fabulous out-of-town shopping centre in Warrington, Cheshire, near where I live, but I fear I may have been scarred for life by one experience I had there. Their Marks & Spencer has a number of entrances and on this particular day I took the exit that I was sure led to my car. You can guess what I didn't find. Cue mounting panic, my thoughts racing. *The car is bright red, so why can't I see it? It* has *to be here*. There was something almost childlike in that feeling of being lost and I felt tears beginning to prick my eyes.

The thing about panic is it makes you increasingly unable to think of new solutions and I kept re-checking the same place, as if I was expecting the car to magically appear; I was unable to think of doing anything else. Of course, the key was simply to STOP PANICKING. I needed to retrace my steps, realise that I'd gone into the shop using a different entrance and – voila! – I found the car.

This approach works, of course, when we lose all sorts of things: we hunt for items in the same place over and over with – guess what? – no success. How many times do we rummage in our bag, insisting that our mobile phone is in there, somewhere, but with no success? STOP doing that, put the kettle on, sit down with a cuppa and think. Visualise the last time you used the phone – who else was there? What were you doing? You get the picture. I promise you will find what you were looking for and faster than getting anyone else to join in on the hunt. Saying that, offering financial incentives to younger members of your family does sometimes result in miracles.

Airports

Heading off for a two-week holiday, my husband Stuart and I booked to park the car at Manchester airport. We followed the instructions very carefully on the map we had been sent of where to leave the vehicle. Back from Tenerife, as we drove out of the car park and through the barrier, we were told we had to pay a whopping £975. Thinking there must have been some mistake – we had prepaid – I queried that with the man on the intercom, who helpfully informed me in a computer-says-no way, 'Sorry, that's what the ticket said, there's nothing I can do.'

Tired after the journey, I paid with a credit card and headed home, thinking I would just deal with it later. When I then went through the paperwork, I discovered that there had been a change in the layout of the airport; the map we had been sent had directed us to what had become the short-stay car park. I sent them the relevant documents, pointed out the problem and I eventually got our money back.

Moral of the story? Airport car parks are without doubt *the* most confusing places on Earth and, if it's 4.30 a.m. and you've got twenty-eight bags with you, you may not spot the subtle differences between zones. In order to claim any money back, you need the tenacity of a pit bull ... but persevere you must – it is your right!!

Flat tyre

We all get them – as I did, many years ago, when I was newly married. I was only about a mile from where we lived and I thought it would be a good idea to return in the car and deal with the problem back home. Suffice to say, that was one of the rare events when Stuart got angry. Who would have known that driving on wheel rims was such a no-no? I guess it will come as no surprise to you to hear that I didn't do that again.

Car wedgie

Having stopped briefly at a service station, I returned to the car, put it into first gear and drove off with purpose through what looked like an empty space ahead of me. I felt a bump, like I'd hit something, and swiftly braked. I got out to see I'd driven over a raised walkway – not a gap – between two parking spaces and the car was now stuck, wedged on top. Had I kept going I would have had enough momentum to make it off. In the end, some nice men took pity on me and lifted the back of my car off the walkway. The vehicle was fine. Sometimes, even the ever-resourceful Jackie Weaver needs rescuing!

> Sometimes, even the ever-resourceful Jackie Weaver needs rescuing!

Tractors and trailers

When I was first married, we lived on my husband's family farm. One day, Stuart asked me if I'd move a trailer, hitching it up to a tractor and driving it down the road into another field. I went ahead and did just that, after which Stuart said, 'Wow – you did that really well. You didn't even look back to check the trailer was going to clear the gate.' Of course, the truth was that I'd completely forgotten about the trailer as I was focusing so much on driving the tractor. How I managed to get that enormous trailer through the gate without so much as a scratch I'll never know.

Middle of nowhere

I've fortunately never broken down far away from civilisation, but I do try to make sure my mobile phone is charged before I head off anywhere and that I have emergency numbers to hand. Letting people know what time to expect you is not only good manners but it means they'll check up on you if you're late. I suppose you could sling a fold-up bike in the back of your car or a spade but admittedly it's not something I do. And if you break down at night and you spot a lone male with a car, be wary: it's not tools he has in the back of his car but more likely a kidnap hood, a syringe he'll use to knock you out and gaffer tape – or perhaps I've been watching too much TV ...

Poor spatial awareness

While I'm a competent driver, I have very poor spatial awareness. When parking the car, I'll look at a car parking space and think, no, my car's not going to fit in there despite the fact there's two white lines that says this is where cars go. So I'll go and find somewhere else. My favourite kind of parking spaces are the 'drive through' ones so that you don't have to reverse. Did I mention that I don't like manoeuvring cars backwards either?

Power cuts

For those times when the electricity goes and you're plunged into darkness, make sure you've stored candles, matches and torches somewhere within easy reach, and perhaps a few blankets to keep you warm. Saying that, what you really want in a power cut is Stuart. Not only does my husband ensure we have a ready supply of batteries for any device (I would go as far to say he has something of a 'battery habit') – but there's nothing he can't make function. In the event of a power cut, the engineer in him would rig something up that would boil water, keep you warm and keep the lights on.

Apocalypse

In an apocalypse – and I've talked to Stuart about this – I would dress up in my best clothes, put my face on, drink some wine and finish off a bottle of pills. I have no wish to live in a post-apocalyptic world – who wants to live on a planet where you can't shop? But Stuart, ever practical, would sort out an electrical source, grow some food, he'd have it all sorted. My view: people would just take it away from you; I'll just stick with my plan. Bit pessimistic? Maybe. I like to think it's about quality of life. For me, a daily struggle to survive is not something I'm willing to do – but if that changes, I'll let you know.

Internet outage

This is my area of household expertise and, when the internet drops out, I'll be the one who figures out why. Usually. But if something goes wrong with the internet or the IT in the house and I can't fix it, I just can't cope. It's more than irritation – it's a feeling that everything in my life that I rely on has suddenly been taken away. I can't even move on to something else – I just have to keep at it, trying to find alternatives to make it work again.

Unemployment

All of the above are, of course, temporary irritants when compared with some of the more serious setbacks we face in life. Losing your job can have major implications for your wellbeing, both in a practical and emotional sense. If it happens, your immediate focus might be on what you've lost. Yes, there is loss – income, principally – but you might have some redundancy money and you'll certainly have time and freedom to consider what to do next. If you really did have the dream job, then it will be all the more tough to say goodbye to it, but the likelihood is that it wasn't – and who knows? You might find something better.

Sometimes losing your job may not have been that unexpected – you may have been pushed but perhaps you were standing at the edge for a long time, wondering whether or not to jump. I know it can be difficult to see it in those terms but if that does sound more like it and you can admit that, you might just be able to turn the potential for negativity into a real opportunity for positive change.

Empty nest

Children growing up and leaving home can make for a real sense of loss. I think the key here is to prepare yourself mentally for the eventuality that your children will one day leave home – and that means making sure you have a life that doesn't solely revolve around them. Some people get entirely wrapped up in their offspring, almost living their lives through them, which I think places too much pressure on those children, making it seem as if they are responsible for the parent's happiness. Even if that is true to a certain extent, children shouldn't feel that pressure – your happiness is not their responsibility.

With my three boys, I always felt they were on loan rather than mine for ever. I brought them up to be independent and able to cope with life without me, which is what you should want for your children. Saying that, a couple of my boys did stay on a bit after eighteen and if we hadn't moved, they might still be with us now! Now, I don't advocate doing a midnight flit or changing the locks but if we make our children feel that we will be miserable without them then perhaps we shouldn't be too surprised if they don't show any signs of establishing their own lives.

> My husband's only criteria when fixing items is whether it works – it doesn't matter if it looks like a pig's ear, as long as it works.

Jackie's confessions

Stuart and I married in 1985. Before he retired, Stuart was a design engineer and, when I met him, he was working on the equipment that printed the security numbers on chequebooks (remember those?!). As a result, Stuart has a real engineer's brain and there is nothing he can't fix. That said, his only criteria when fixing items is whether it works – it doesn't matter if it looks like a pig's ear, as long as it works (and, to be honest, maybe he's right).

> We met through a blind date arranged by mutual
> work colleagues and our first son was born a year after
> we married. We went on to have another two boys
> and all have now grown up and flown the nest. We
> sold the family farm six years ago and moved. It's back
> to just me and Stuart now, but I think we make a very
> happy team.

When the worst happens

At some point in our lives we all lose someone dear to us;
the pain and sadness we go through can be seriously
distressing. In the early stages of bereavement, it is common
for people to imagine the whole of their life ahead as being
empty without their loved ones in it. Far better, if you can,
in these early days of grief, to focus on getting through the
day – worry about tomorrow tomorrow. If you look too
far ahead, you're not going to make accommodation for
the fact that your emotions and circumstances will change
over time. None of us are the same person we were five
years ago. To begin with, just congratulate yourself for
making it through the day and if that means being in your
pyjamas today then so be it – tomorrow may be different.

I should have . . .

One of the things that makes loss or bereavement so difficult to deal with is that you can no longer have the conversation you feel you should have had with that person. In

that case, why don't you have that conversation or say those words now? Tell the people you hold dear that you love them. If you're angry as hell when you set off for work in the morning, tell your partner that you're really mad, but that there's no time to talk about it now *and* you still love them. I'm not talking about great big doorstep speeches whenever you say, 'Goodbye,' but don't leave with an atmosphere – make sure the people you love know how you feel.

Arm yourself

In navigating this thing called life, expect the unexpected: you will one day get lost in an airport car park; you might experience the car equivalent of a wedgie at a service station and there will be moments in your life when you have no power or means to charge your phone (imagine that?). But we can prepare for those eventualities, keep calm when they happen and arm ourselves for those really difficult setbacks. It won't necessarily make them any less painful but you might feel a smidgeon better if you have told your loved ones exactly what they meant to you, or that your grown-up children, who might not be heading up a FTSE-500 company just yet, are none-theless leading happy and independent lives. In short:

Expect life to be full of adversity

Don't panic if something goes wrong or you've lost something – visualise

Read signs very carefully at airport car parks!

Demand money back if you've been charged unfairly – be tenacious!

Your children are not responsible for your happi-ness – you are

If you're newly grieving, just focus on getting through the day

Tell those you hold dear you love them as often as possible

Chapter Nine

A Commonsense Approach: Embrace the Ordinary

What is the point of drawing up a
fantastic list of things you want to do, if
you get run over by a bus tomorrow?

I'd like to think I employ a commonsense and practical approach in much of what I do and – despite (*ahem*) being something of a megastar now in these parts – I keep my feet firmly on the ground. Having common sense, though, does not preclude enjoying life: I certainly try to make the most of every day and will, if the situation presents itself, have a little fun along the way.

I'm also a firm believer in getting on with life – don't save the best for later; do those things you've been meaning to do and show a bit of love to the people who matter. And don't be so wrapped up in yourself or your busy day to stop noticing the things around you that actually make you happy, some of which might be very ordinary but nonetheless give you a bit of a lift.

Where shall we start? Well, somebody said (Benjamin Franklin, was it? Or Brad Pitt?) that in this world nothing can be certain except death and taxes. Let's not get into taxes – although, let's face it, they're pretty crucial in the parish council world – but, yes, life is finite: it will end and, for that reason, you need just to get on and do the things you want to do *now*! Here are a few other commonsense tips for life.

The exceptions that prove the rules

There are a host of rules or maxims that we all think we must follow in life when common sense says otherwise!

Bucket lists

What's this thing with bucket lists? If there's something you want to do, don't wait, just do it. What is the point of drawing up a fantastic list of things you're looking forward to doing, if you get run over by a bus tomorrow?

And why wait for the day when you miraculously have a ton of money before you do anything on your bucket list? If you asked most people what they would do if they won a million pounds, I bet there would be things on that list that would cost next to nothing. If there are things that you've always wanted to do and they're important to you, do them now. None of us are getting any younger!

Save the best for later

Again, what are you waiting for? Wear those shoes and that dress and drag those crystal glasses out from the back of the cupboard. If they give you pleasure, get them out now. Perhaps there's a voice in your head that's saying you're not worthy of them? Who *would* you get the best glasses and plates out for? Maybe that's a conversation you need to have with yourself? Make your own rules about these things – don't be bound by those of others. In my head, I can still hear my mother's voice and to this day I still can't wear blue shoes with a black dress or vice versa.

You always hurt the one you love

Really? What do you do to people you *don't* like? The line came from a popular song sung by men to 'explain' why they cheat. Don't buy into it. The last person you should hurt is the one you love and if they hurt you, trust me – they don't love you!

> # The last person you should hurt is the one you love and if they hurt you, trust me – they don't love you!

Green fingers

Having 'green fingers' simply means you prioritise the care of your plants over other things. Your plants die because you forget to water them. You wouldn't forget to feed your children! It's all about priorities and if you don't have time to water your plants, don't buy them (and note, if you do forget to feed or water your children we will hear about it)!

We all want choice

Why is it that supermarkets think we all want more and more choice? I shop like a ninja – in, target, sight, buy, out. I don't want to walk half a mile across a vast car park and then do another mile around the aisles, desperately looking for an assistant or cornflakes. I don't do giant supermarkets; I try to shop locally – there are lots of good reasons to do so – and I feel I am saving the planet too. And is it me or have you noticed that the smaller the supermarket, the larger the car parking spaces?

Pay it forward

I like to be polite. Even when writing a text message, I'm one of those people who will add lots of 'pleases' and 'thank-yous', along with full stops and capitals in the right place, and will always sign off with 'kind regards, Jackie'. I just can't help myself!

In the same way, if I'm out and about and someone says to me, 'Ooh, your nails are nice,' I'm really chuffed by that and I like to pay that forward. When I'm paying for my shopping at the till, I'll say a little something, such as, 'Gosh, it looks like it's been busy today,' just to demonstrate that I see the cashier as a human being and more than just their role as checkout operator.

Those small exchanges really make a difference. When the Handforth parish council meeting went viral, I was incredibly touched by people I knew who got in touch just to say, 'Are you OK?' It meant a great deal to me.

> When the Handforth story went viral, I was incredibly touched by people I knew who got in touch just to say, 'Are you OK?' It meant a great deal to me.

Inspirational quotes

Many of us like to have motivational quotes around the house – perhaps in the form of fridge magnets. But how many of us really take them on board? You might have, tucked behind that shopping list, something really meaningful, like, 'When you stop expecting people to be perfect, you can like them for who they are.' Think about what that means and go action it!

One of my favourite inspirational quotes is: 'If the shoe fits, buy it in every colour.' That's one I've definitely taken on board (oh, and if there is a matching bag – well, why not?).

Jackie's confessions

Some people keep grounded by walking somewhere rural or taking in a view. I have to confess, I'm not one of those people. I'm really not lying when I say I have no interest in geography! It's the plants in my own garden that keep me connected to the world. Many of them have an emotional connection to my life and I take pleasure in watching them grow. We have walnut and fig trees and an old dwarf apple tree brought from our farmhouse along with a dwarf lilac that my mother-in-law bought us over thirty years ago when we were newly married.

We also have a monkey puzzle tree that, since the early 1990s, has grown from being four feet to fifteen feet high. When Stuart and I look at it – and don't get me wrong, we don't go out every night and worship it – we are always aware that we could never grow that tree again. It was so slow-growing and we know we wouldn't live long enough to see it through. It's not something I get terrifically sad about but it's a reminder that life charges on and we've got more behind us than in front.

Don't say, 'No' when you mean 'Yes'

Don't say – and I'm afraid I think women are more guilty of this than men – 'No, I don't want anything special for my birthday' when, in fact, you know you'll be hurt if you are taken at your word. If I said that to my husband, well, I just wouldn't get anything. Women tend to 'hint' they want something, but the problem is their other halves may not be very good on picking up on those subtleties!

My husband isn't the only reason I'm fairly direct in the way I speak. At the age of three, one of my sons hadn't started talking. Various health visitors and medics thought he might be deaf, but I knew he wasn't. It turned out he had a form of autism and at that age he couldn't manage the complexity of language. If I said, 'Just pop upstairs and get your orange socks out of the blue bin and take them to your dad,' he would just stand there, not having assimilated what I'd asked him to do. If I said, 'Orange socks . . . blue bin . . . take them to Dad,' he'd go and do it. I learned to pare down what I said to the bare essentials – and sometimes that's a very useful skill to have in life!

So often we attribute mind-reading skills to the people who are around us and then we are disappointed when they get it wrong.

Stop saying 'should'

Look at the number of times you say 'should': I should eat more vegetables, I should phone so-and-so. Why *should* you

– and have you noticed that whenever you say 'should', it doesn't happen? Swap 'should' with 'I will' or 'I want to' and then you can figure out if you really want to do those things. And if you are still left with 'should', perhaps you need to let it go – stop beating yourself up for not doing whatever it is.

Embrace the ordinary

How many of us enjoy coming home when we've been away on holiday? The food has been amazing, but then you started looking forward to toast. And nowhere abroad can you get as good a cup of tea as you can at home.

Don't overlook how much your everyday life means to you – pause a while and take time to notice the things around you that mean the most. Some of the little things in my life that give me pleasure are my two dogs, Izzy and Rosie. Izzy, in particular, has slightly goofy front teeth and a bit of an overbite and seeing those little white teeth always makes me smile. She also has bat-like ears that move around and are wonderfully expressive in themselves. Is she well-behaved? Heck, no – but she is very sweet!

Soap-opera life

Good relationships don't have to come with the drama that we see on the small screen. We don't have to shout and fight to show we care. Positive relationships can also be calm, loving and supportive without the excitement. It doesn't mean your relationship is less worthwhile, it just means that it doesn't need a TV crew to make it work. The drama might work for thirty minutes on the screen, but imagine a life like that? I know it's not for me.

Best mum or dad in the world

It's enough to be a good parent – we don't all have to be a perfect parent. Birthday cards, magazines and the media tell us we must be the greatest at bringing up our kids and while we strive to live up to that, we're missing out on the joy of simply being enough: a person who cares for, nurtures and loves their children. That's all you need to do and be.

Life really is too short to dust skirting boards.

Life's too short

I like to keep a clean house, will happily iron tea towels, pillowcases and the like, but there are some things I draw the line at. Life really is too short to . . .

. . . dust skirting boards – why would you unless you have very small people in your house?

. . . pair socks – why not let your family express their creativity by wearing any socks they like!

... stuff a mushroom – but maybe someone else said that one!

Life is too short to write a bucket list – live it. You *will* get older. You *will* make mistakes: perfection is an ideal not an aspiration. Good enough is good enough. You *should* and you *could* but it will only happen if you *want*. Mind-readers are in short supply: you are ordinary and that is fabulous.

Design for life

I hope you appreciate a few of my home-truths, all born from having a commonsense and, some might say, no-nonsense approach to life. Life does not need to be full of drama and sometimes it's the small and ordinary things that we delight in the most.

Say 'YES' to:

    Getting on with life – do the stuff you want to do

    Telling your loved ones how you feel

    Complimenting other people

    Being polite

    Stating clearly what you want

    Taking time to notice things around you

    Being a good parent, not the best in the world

Say 'NO' to:

    Writing a bucket list

    Saving the best for later

    Being vague and hinting what you want

    Saying I 'should'

    A relationship full of drama

    Dusting skirting boards

Chapter Ten

Be Comfortable In Your Own Skin

We are constantly told we are unique and special – in
all likelihood, we are neither of those things.

The media bombards us with messages that we are unique and special. That's a lot to live up to. You may be lovely or a little different, but I doubt you're unique or truly extraordinary. And why are you yearning to be so very special anyway?

Think about how we build a house. What if all the bricks were different and special in their own way? Could you build a home with them? Probably not! In society, we need to work together to build things that are greater than the individual and we are more alike than we are different.

That drive towards uniqueness also feeds into the desire for perfection: we strive for the perfect hair, partner, family, lifestyle and we feel inadequate if we can't attain it. And yet, once you've achieved that goal weight or captured that perfect man, might life have passed you by in the process? Yes, you can work on improving what you've got – and, God help me, I've tried over the years – but in the long run, there needs to be some acceptance of who we are because – well, who else have we got?

As someone who has struggled with weight my whole life, I very much understand that internal voice that says something like, 'I'll do that when I am thin,' but the scary thing is that, in the meantime, our lives are passing us by. The reality is that, whoever we are, we can still live a great life – but we need to believe that.

Figure out who you are

In the early years of my marriage, I remember always being introduced as 'Stuart Weaver's wife' or 'Michael Weaver's mother' etc – almost as if I didn't have my own identity and existed only in relation to another person. I know that I would handle the situation very differently now, as the person I am today. I think my work and the passing years have helped me to find that identity and really figure out who I am. And that helps me to feel more confident, which feeds into my sense of authority.

Ageing

Of course, accepting who you are means getting to grips with ageing – an inevitable process that you can either accept or fight against (and who do you think will be the winner in that contest?). If your whole identity is bound up in youth and beauty, you may well have a problem. But if your identity is able to evolve with the years, then ageing itself can come with all sorts of benefits. Here are just a handful I've discovered:

You no longer worry about people thinking you're making a pass at them (nowadays they're more likely to think I'm trying to adopt them!).

You are less concerned about what people think of you. Of course, this can vary from person to person, but in my experience, what might have felt like the most embarrassing thing in the world when I was younger is water off a duck's back to the older me.

You no longer feel the need (or perhaps don't have the strength) to be unique and special. It takes off a lot of pressure. This is such an important point that it really cannot be emphasised enough. If you are unique and special, that's great – I don't say you should hide that – but if you are ordinary then that shouldn't be seen as second best – it is not.

And the disadvantages of being older?

As soon as you reach a certain age, you're grouped into a particular demographic and people make certain assumptions. I remember a young council officer giving a presentation in which she referred to the over-fifties as a vulnerable group – clearly envisaging people in wheel-chairs and using Stannah stairlifts, unable to shop or prepare their five-a-day. How on earth can you make such assumptions about such a massive demographic group? At sixty I'm still the one providing, in many ways, for the younger members of our family. I'm certainly not the one in the bath chair being fed!

Women, in particular, can feel invisible after a certain age and, to a certain extent, that's true. I know quite a few women in positions of power who might fall into this category; who may not be turning heads in the way they might have once done. This does beg the question: do you need to be visible to be powerful?

For women of a certain age – and men, too, for that matter – the availability of toilets when away from home becomes a real issue. Bladder control is perhaps not what it once was (my trampolining days are definitely over) and bowel movements may be non-existent or – well, a little sudden . . . which is not much fun if there isn't a toilet in sight!

How to get your man

You would think we'd have moved on from this kind of language but, unbelievably, you still see articles and books about 'getting your man', 'how to keep him happy' when you've got him and 'how to get him back' if you've lost him. What made men the centre of women's worlds? If you can't be yourself when you are with a man – or any partner, come to that – walk away. And if you pretend to be something else to get your man, how long can you keep that up and will it make you happy? Where are *you* in all of this?

Do you think men read articles about 'how to get your girl'? I somehow doubt it. The message for men seems to be 'be yourself' – I totally agree with that, but I also think that that should be good enough for us girls too.

Diets

How many of us strive for that perfect weight or think we'll be that much happier if we're just a few pounds lighter? The problem is we often think to ourselves: I'm miserable and fat and, if I lose weight, I will no longer be miserable and fat. No, you'll be miserable and thin because you've not actually addressed what was making you miserable. All you've done is focus on the challenge of losing weight – which you might enjoy – but that is not necessarily the answer. Sometimes you need to work on your own self-worth and what it is that is making you unhappy.

I've had my own battles with dieting and, over the years, my weight has fluctuated by six stone. In fact, when my children were small, I used to be a Slimming World advisor and ran several groups very successfully. I remember being able to tell who was in the right frame of mind; when you want to lose weight more than anything else, it's not complicated. But if you feel you *should* lose weight – and not that you will or *want to* lose weight – you might as well try pulling your own teeth out as it's not going to happen.

If I was in the mood myself, I could lose weight very easily – as much as five stone (almost thirty-two kilograms) in six months. But then, even when I was at my thinnest, I still didn't feel things were right; I'd hold on to that weight-loss with my fingertips, only for the pounds to inevitably creep back on again.

There was a time when I thought, It doesn't matter what I do in the wider world, I'm still fat, therefore it doesn't count for anything. It's an attitude that I think was shaped by my mother, who was stick-thin and always made a point of telling me I was not – and she wasn't subtle, using such delightful phrases as 'fat pig'.

So ingrained was this feeling that I remember going into a plus-size shop (not the shop itself, that was the same size as all the other shops, it just sold plus-size clothes!) and the assistant said that she didn't think they'd have anything in my size. My immediate thought was that I was too big – in fact, I was too small, as I'd just lost a lot of weight.

To this day I avoid mirrors, although I'm more accepting about my weight and body type overall. I might try to lose the odd pound or two, but my weight no longer defines who I am and I know that being thinner does not neces-sarily result in instant happiness. And, to be honest, I no longer want to go through that weekly rigmarole – which my husband also has had to live with. I would weigh myself on a Monday morning and, despite having restricted myself from everything the week before, I wouldn't have lost anything or would have even gained weight – and then I'd be miserable all week.

> I recognise that I'm never going to have model proportions, no matter how thin I am – although I do sometimes look at really small women with a pang of envy and think, where do they keep their giblets?

Skincare

Airbrushing, filters and soft-focus lenses have a lot to answer for.

Our heroes and heroines appear to have perfect skin, devoid of wrinkles or blemishes, providing an ideal by which we all have to measure ourselves. We might pay lip service to the phrase, 'Beauty is only skin deep', but I'm not sure we really believe it, as we keep buying those products that we hope will release our inner beauty (me included)!

I have very dry skin and I've always spent quite a lot on various oils and creams as I felt my skin needed it. During the pandemic, however, when many of our normal routines went out of the window, I stopped bothering. And do you know what? My skin wasn't any worse than it was before – if anything it seemed to benefit from less attention. I wonder now whether the products we put on in turn require us to put on other lotions and potions? Saying that, if you enjoy the luxury brands and they make you feel good and cared for, then buy them, but I'm not sure they're absolutely necessary. If any of the brands want to convince me otherwise, you can contact me via Twitter . . .

Hair

OK . . . hair is another minefield. Models in adverts look that good because (A) they're models and (B) they've had their hair professionally styled for several hours before anyone gets near a camera and (C) the whole image is retouched to within an inch of its life before it is released to the wider public. Which is why, of course, when you're slapping on the same product at home and then giving your hair a quick blast while making toast, the results are not quite so impressive.

Similarly, for those of us who are older and whose role models are more like Joan Collins or Jane Fonda – let me tell you no woman of that age has lush hair and if she appears to have long and gorgeous locks then it's probably not real.

All the same, I do like to get my hair done, but I'm fairly realistic about the likely result. I'm not going to come out of the hairdresser with such fabulous hair that literally people will stop me in the street. Nor is it going to be so bloody awful that people won't want to see me or I'll need a bag over my head. I'm hoping for something in between.

Overheard at the hairdressers

Hairdresser: OK, so what are we going for this time?

You: Just the same as last time.

(How many clients do you think he or she has seen since you last came in?! Do you think they can remember exactly how you have your hair every time?)

Hairdresser: Which side parting you do you have?

Me: Well, this side but, to be honest, the world will still turn if you put it on the other side.

You: I want something completely different *but* please don't take anything off the length, I don't want it thinning, I don't like the parting on the other side and I don't want the colour changing. But, apart from that – I'm in your hands.

Hairdresser: ???

Jackie's confessions

I used to have a habit of twiddling my hair – a favourite piece on the front, a single tress, carefully teased out from the other and gently pulled through two fingers – which my mother couldn't stand. One day, when I was about fourteen, she grabbed a pair of scissors and cut off the bit of hair I was twirling. Even now I can still vividly remember that moment of mental disconnect as I held the hair in my hand, trying to compute what had just happened. And then I had to suffer the embarrassment of going to school with a strange tuft of hair at the front. Even today, I still try not to twirl my hair because I think it might annoy Stuart – of course, it doesn't and he'd anyway be more concerned that I was stressed about something.

It really is amazing how these things can have such a lasting impact on you – and it goes without saying the incident did nothing to improve the relationship I had with my mother.

Happy families

Talking of perfect families, the definition of what makes one is constantly changing. But, of course, the truth is that there really is no such thing as a perfect family. Sometimes we perceive one family or another as ideal – they look fantastic, have an amazing car, the kids seem to be destined for greatness – but we have no understanding of what is being sacrificed to make them perfect. What's going on behind that front door? Perhaps they all argue just as much as we do at mealtimes but they've had the presence of mind to install double-glazing.

Nobody is perfect

One thing you do learn as you get older is that everyone has their own insecurities or weaknesses – people might look like they're super-confident or in total control of their lives, but rarely is that the case. It's how you manage yourself that counts. Amazing as it may seem, I do have weaknesses, but I simply accept them and play to my strengths – I could work harder on my weaknesses, but, well, I choose not to . . .

My weaknesses:

I'm not very good at coping with other people's emotions.

I'm not interested in nature, geography, history or the lives of people I don't know. People think I'm kidding when I say that but I'm just not!

I'm never going to be Britney Spears.

I should learn to speak Spanish and should be better at maths – there's that *should* again – but I'm not really putting much effort in, so I don't think it's ever going to happen.

My strengths:

I'm good at seeing the connections between things. At work, I'll have a conversation with one person and then another and will often think, Yep, you two need to get together. They do and good things comes as a result.

I like to solve problems and can see how various scenarios might unfold. That's the problem with the children running the country – they come up with a plan, but they don't ask the next question, 'And then what?' In contrast, I'm always going over in my mind what might happen afterwards and will have already thought through the worst-case scenarios.

I'm kind and I don't think kindness is valued enough. You can have authority and power, but you need also to be a decent human being and, in my book, that means being kind. It is often the small kindnesses we do for others that we are remembered for.

Being happy

For me, being comfortable in your own skin is about being happy. It's not about striving for total perfection in your life and proving to everyone else how fantastic, unique and special you are. Having great hair or losing a bit of weight might give you a bit of a boost but it won't instantly make you happy. Be kind but don't lose your identity in the service of others – stand up for yourself and accept the good and bad. In short, remember:

- You are not unique, special or perfect and that is absolutely fine
- A good relationship is one in which you can be yourself
- You will age – get over it
- Remember that hairdressers cannot perform miracles (but cameras can)
- Losing weight is not the only answer to happiness
- Play to your strengths and manage your weaknesses

Chapter Eleven

The Final Word

*I'm all for animal welfare but no amount of
sympathy for donkeys with wonky feet is going
to make the donkeys feel any better.*

Our front garden looks as if my husband Stuart and I have
a serious drinking problem. The number of cans we have
outside our front door is frightening and, as there's probably every type of can on display, it would seem we have no
brand loyalty either.

The reality is that, when Stuart takes the dogs for a walk
and spots any cans in the hedge (perhaps lying alongside
those blasted poo bags), he'll pick them up, bring them
home and we'll recycle them. Will that small deed save the
world? No. But if ten thousand other people did the same,
it would certainly make a difference.

People are often overwhelmed by the feeling that issues
or problems in the world are just too big for one person to

tackle. But you can make a difference where you live – within your community – that can be really rewarding and of tangible benefit to you and your neighbours. If you make small changes first, you're more likely to be successful and then you can build on that achievement and perhaps other people will join you.

My world is, of course, parish and town councils, but the principle of starting small can apply to all sorts of organisations, from schools or churches to large companies. Parish councils come in all sizes and cover very different geographical areas, from town centres to deeply rural places where there are more sheep than people. They have budgets ranging from a couple of thousand to a couple of million. But the problem – one of my biggest frustrations – is that principal authorities try to design or make a service work for every type of parish council. But it's difficult – if not sometimes impossible – to come up with a one-size-fits-all plan; we never get past discussing the policy, can't get the plan right, and often end up doing nothing.

My argument is, why not do something small, rather than nothing at all, and then build on that success and engage other people? An example of this in the work I do: an authority announced they had too many buildings and they wanted local town and parish councils to take over ownership of them. Rather than working endlessly on a policy that would be suitable for every council off the shelf, we started with one town hall and one council. The town hall, under the subsequent ownership of the local council, was revamped as a venue for weddings, indoor bowls and dancing – that kind of thing – and they opened a café and some offices. It became a viable and thriving business. Local people were invested in the project and it became clear just what could be done. As soon as we could show what was possible, other councils began to question why they couldn't do the same – and they did.

Why not do something small, rather than nothing at all, and then build on that success and engage other people?

What's this got to do with changing the world? Well, starting with the small things is a good principle to follow in life and can apply to every topic we've covered in this book. We sometimes try to overhaul our lives completely when in fact often we need only to make small changes.

To keep on track during a meeting or in a difficult conversation, focus on what you want to achieve, keep it simple and don't try to take on everything at once. To be assertive, you first need to be clear in your mind about what you want and you're far more likely to be heard if you talk about one or two things on your agenda rather than rant on about everything.

If you're overwhelmed with a busy to-do-list, deal with things one at a time, lifting each lid on those imaginary boxes. Concentrate and congratulate yourself for simply getting through the day if you're dealing with really serious issues or major setbacks and don't focus on the enormity of the whole of your life. And sometimes it's just the small everyday things that can give you the most pleasure – from your dog's goofy teeth to that plant you've miraculously never killed. And, while you might want to work on your weaknesses, it's your strengths you should highlight.

The key to all of this, of course, is knowing that it's more important to do *something* than it is to do everything. You might change something locally and it could be something very small but, if it matters to you, do something about it. And don't kid yourself that simply telling people about it or sharing pictures on social media is enough.

I know someone who regularly posts images on Facebook showing various types of animal cruelty. I got so fed up with it that I ended up asking the person what *they* were doing about it, as animal welfare was clearly a critical issue. They needed to do something practical themselves: rescue a donkey, buy a meerkat, whatever. Just don't send me stuff hoping to guilt-trip me into action. I mean, I'm all for animal welfare but no amount of sympathy for donkeys with wonky feet is going to make the donkeys feel any better. If you really care about something, then do something positive – virtue signalling is not going to make the lives of our four-legged friends any easier.

Donkeys aside, I guess you can probably tell I'm a pragmatist: I want to tackle issues, fix problems in the short and long term and not just talk. I'm also a firm believer in the rules, born, I think, from having a strong moral compass. If I think something is unfair – and that could be anything from someone getting belittled or overlooked at work to a random couple being charged an eye-wateringly large car-park fine – I feel compelled to do something about it. Life is messy and I like to create order or at least try to make sense of the challenges we all face. And those traits – my own standing orders if you like – have carried me through life and given me all the authority I need.

Finally, thank you for buying my book – if you have read all the way to here, then thank you for the time you have spent with me. And if you put any of my thoughts into practice, I would really love to hear how they went for you.